The media's wat
Here's a samplin  ~verage.

"For those hoping to climb the ladder of success, [Vault's] insights are priceless."
– *Money magazine*

"The best place on the web to prepare for a job search."
– *Fortune*

"[Vault guides] make for excellent starting points for job hunters and should be purchased by academic libraries for their career sections [and] university career centers."
– *Library Journal*

"The granddaddy of worker sites."
– *US News and World Report*

"A killer app."
– *New York Times*

One of Forbes' 33 "Favorite Sites"
– *Forbes*

"To get the unvarnished scoop, check out Vault."
– *Smart Money Magazine*

"Vault has a wealth of information about major employers and job-searching strategies as well as comments from workers about their experiences at specific companies."
– *The Washington Post*

"A key reference for those who want to know what it takes to get hired by a law firm and what to expect once they get there."
– *New York Law Journal*

"Vault [provides] the skinny on working conditions at all kinds of companies from current and former employees."
– *USA Today*

VAULT GUIDE TO CAPITOL HILL CAREERS

VAULT GUIDE TO CAPITOL HILL CAREERS

**WILLIAM MCCARTHY
AND THE STAFF OF VAULT**

Library of Congress Cataloging-in-Publication Data

McCarthy, William, 1969-
  Vault guide to Capitol Hill careers / William McCarthy and the staff of Vault.
    p. cm.
  ISBN 1-58131-251-2 (alk. paper)
  1. United States. Congress--Officials and employees--Vocational guidance. 2. Interns (Legislation)--Vocational guidance--United States. 3. Lobbying--Vocational guidance--United States. 4. Public relations--Vocational guidance--United States. 5. Mass media--Vocational guidance--United States. I. Vault (Firm) II. Title.
  JK1083.M35 2003
  328.73'0023--dc21

                                                                        2003008380

Printed in the United States of America

ACKNOWLEDGEMENTS

From Bill McCarthy: To my wife Abby, for all her inspiration and support, and to all those who shared their experiences and guided my thinking on this project.

From Vault: Thanks to Matt Doull, Ahmad Al-Khaled, Lee Black, Eric Ober, Hollinger Ventures, Tekbanc, New York City Investment Fund, Globix, Hoover's, Glenn Fischer, Mark Hernandez, Ravi Mhatre, Carter Weiss, Ken Cron, Ed Somekh, Isidore Mayrock, Zahi Khouri, Sana Sabbagh, and other Vault investors, as well as our family and friends.

Table of Contents

Visit Vault at **www.vault.com** for insider company profiles, expert advice,
career message boards, expert resume reviews, the Vault Job Board and more.

VAULT CAREER
LIBRARY

xi

Introduction

Washington, DC offers one of the most unique and exciting job markets in the world. This book examines careers that are specific to the nation's capital, with an eye toward identifying entry points, career paths, and insider advice for those with a strong desire for a career in politics, government and all that Washington has to offer.

For many new to Washington, their careers will begin on Capitol Hill. The offices of the nation's 100 Senators and 435 Representatives have been the training grounds for many of history's most influential staffers, power brokers, and political Svengalis. Capitol Hill offers a virtual immersion program into all aspects of government and politics.

The path to the top ranks of Washington's political and governmental elite, however, usually begins with menial tasks for low pay. A staff assistant on Capitol Hill, the typical entry-level position for someone with a Bachelor's degree, earns as little as $20,000 regardless of the prestige of his or her alma mater. First assignments include answering the phones, staffing the front desk, and even fetching lunch for the boss – not exactly the glamorous lifestyle portrayed by television or the movies.

With time and experience, however a world of opportunity opens to those with the desire and stamina to pursue it. With the right combination of ambition, learning, and contacts, those who once helped answer the phones can soon help shepherd major pieces of legislation to the floor of the U.S. House of Representatives or spin public policy to a reporter for *The Washington Post*.

Beyond Capitol Hill, a host of opportunities await. While many people begin their careers on Capitol Hill, even more look beyond the House and Senate offices to equally exciting and interesting positions focused on national politics, government, issue advocacy, and international affairs. To excel in any of these positions, it is not necessary to work for Congress (but it certainly can help). And the fact is that most Capitol Hill staffers will not finish their careers on the Hill. The overwhelming majority of Hill staffers are not lifers; they work for a period of time and then pursue other opportunities that leverage their experiences.

Additionally, Washington, DC respects and rewards those with advanced degrees. The nation's capital has always been a lawyer's town, and many of the top Congressional staff members, lobbyists, and government officials hold law degrees. Masters in Public Policy are valued within the legislative

Looking for a new challenge? The Vault Job Board has thousands of top jobs for all experience levels. Visit www.vault.com.

VAULT CAREER LIBRARY   1

and policy community. And Washington is gaining newfound life for master's in Business Administration holders as the government, public policy, and non-profit sectors of the city's economy awake to the benefits of the degree. In George W. Bush, the United States has elected its first MBA President, and several of his top Cabinet Members, such as Secretary of Labor Elaine Chao and Secretary of Commerce Don Evans, hold MBAs.

While education is important, Washington values personal networks and experience above all else. Therefore, the best way to begin a career in Washington is by amassing both as early as possible. This book will guide you through the process of beginning and advancing your future Washington, DC career to fulfill your goals, whatever they might be.

A myriad of career paths

While this book covers many of the career possibilities – both in and out of government - in the nation's capital, most Washingtonians do not stick strictly with one career path. In fact, a look back at the careers of many high level Washington professionals shows career trajectories that zigzag among government, political, and private sector work. Therefore, anyone considering a career in Washington should not feel locked in to just one area of expertise.

One of the great advantages of working in Washington is the opportunity to parlay experience in one career area into other interesting and exciting areas. It is not at all unusual to meet a former attorney now serving as a communications director to a high-level official, for example, or a businessperson who now heads up a national political committee. Washington values intelligence, loyalty, and the ability to get things done, and those traits translate across many types of experiences and job functions.

Often, the most intimidating part of building a career in Washington is simply getting started. There are many entry-level positions for people of all educational levels, as this book illustrates. Once a newcomer to Washington begins to build a network of contacts and establishes a track record of success, new paths are likely to open, including many unseen at the beginning of the journey. Therefore, one of the best ways to build your career in Washington, DC is to participate in the life of the city itself, which is unique among major American cities.

However, since there are so many potential career paths, there is no way for this book to outline every possible option available throughout the metropolitan region. Therefore, it focuses only on those that should prove to be the most interesting and unique to the readers. Most of the book focuses on opportunities on Capitol Hill and in the political realm of Washington, DC Why? Because that is where the action is and they are at the heart of what makes Washington unique. However, there are other interesting opportunities available to those with advanced degrees outside of Capitol Hill, and some potential options for law school graduates and MBAs are also covered.

Although this book is divided by academic degrees, it is worthwhile to read the entire book. A description of a career path in one section may someday be of interest to an MBA working in international finance, as would the opportunities in community development that are available to MBAs possibly be of interest to an undergraduate just beginning his or her career on Capitol Hill. The Washington, DC region has a tremendous amount to offer in terms of unique career opportunities, and this book should help you get started.

Visit Vault at **www.vault.com** for insider company profiles, expert advice, career message boards, expert resume reviews, the Vault Job Board and more.

VAULT CAREER LIBRARY

3

Use the Internet's
MOST TARGETED
job search tools.

Vault Job Board

Target your search by industry, function, and experience level, and find the job openings that you want.

VaultMatch Resume Database

Vault takes match-making to the next level: post your resume and customize your search by industry, function, experience and more. We'll match job listings with your interests and criteria and e-mail them directly to your inbox.

> the most trusted name in career information™

THE SCOOP

Chapter 2: Welcome to Washington

Chapter 3: Inside Capitol Hill

Visit Vault at **www.vault.com** for insider company profiles, expert advice,
career message boards, expert resume reviews, the Vault Job Board and more.

VAULT CAREER LIBRARY

5

Losing sleep over your job search?
Endlessly revising your resume?
Facing a work-related dilemma?

Super-charge your career with Vault's newest career tools: Resume Reviews, Resume Writing and Career Coaching.

Vault Resume Writing

On average, a hiring manager weeds through 120 resumes for a single job opening. Let our experts write your resume from scratch to make sure it stands out.

- Start with an e-mailed history and 1- to 2-hour phone discussion
- Vault experts will create a first draft
- After feedback and discussion, Vault experts will deliver a final draft, ready for submission

Vault Resume Review

- Submit your resume online
- Receive an in-depth e-mailed critique with suggestions on revisions within TWO BUSINESS DAYS

Vault Career Coach

Whether you are facing a major career change or dealing with a workplace dilemma, our experts can help you make the most educated decision via telephone counseling sessions.

- Sessions are 45-minutes over the telephone

For more information go to
www.vault.com/careercoach

V∧ULT
> the most trusted name in career information™

Welcome to Washington

CHAPTER 2

Why Washington?

The nation's capital is an exciting, dynamic, international city. It is also a transient city. Every year, thousands of recent graduates swarm the region looking to break into a career in government and politics. At the same time, many others will leave to return home or pursue opportunities elsewhere after deciding that the pressure and the raw ambitions so obviously displayed are not for them.

Washington's transience and youth give the city, at times, the feeling of a college campus. It is a city literally bursting with energy from neighborhoods as diverse as Capitol Hill and Dupont Circle in the District, to Clarendon and Ballston in Arlington County, Virginia and Bethesda, Maryland. In these and other areas, the region caters to young, educated elites who come with their diplomas and ambitions in hand.

Washington has multiple identities. First and foremost, Washington is a government town. As the seat of the Federal government, the District of Columbia plays host to countless employees who staff the executive, legislative and judicial branches of government. Within the District are the most powerful institutions of our government: The White House and the Cabinet Agencies, the United States Congress, and the United States Supreme Court. The Federal government gives Washington its most notable characteristic – above all else, politics rules Washington. From the parlors of Georgetown to the dive bars of Capitol Hill, politics is the city's obsession. Nearly every aspect of professional life in the city is viewed through a political lens. Political staffers whose jobs depend on the party or individual in power obsess over politics for good reason. So do the lobbyists and lawyers who work every day on Federal policy. Politics is sport in Washington.

Washington is also an academic city. It is home to many national colleges and universities. Georgetown University, George Washington University, American University, and Catholic University are located within the District's boundaries. The University of Maryland is in suburban Washington and the University of Virginia is a two-hour drive away. As home to many of the world's most prestigious think tanks, Washington hosts some of the nation's prominent scholars. While it is fairly well known that Washington has the highest number of lawyers per capita of any city in the country, there is also a good chance that the young waitress who serves your dinner has just received her PhD in international affairs, and is biding her time until she finds the right position. The people attracted to Washington are usually well educated and want to put their higher learning to use on behalf of a cause, ideology, or for their own ambitions.

The diplomatic license plates that dot the capital's highways and side streets are an ongoing reminder that Washington is also a very international city. The city is home to countless foreign embassies and is, naturally, a destination for many foreign dignitaries. Many of the government relations firms and public affairs agencies in the nation's capital do extensive business with foreign clients. The international flavor of the city also provides unique – only-in-Washington – opportunities on the social scene. Events like embassy parties allow you to travel to foreign soil (embassies and their grounds are governed by their home country) by the Washington Metro.

The cultural opportunities in the Washington region are virtually unmatched anywhere in America based on the sheer number of museums, exhibits, concerts, plays, and festivals and their easy accessibility. Many cultural opportunities are offered free to the public, including admission the Smithsonian, the National Gallery of Art, and various festivals and displays throughout the city and region. People new to the city often choose to explore the cultural scene – and expand their social spheres – by becoming members in one or more of the exceptional small art galleries located in Washington, including the Corcoran and the Phillips Collection.

All of these factors, plus many more, combine to make Washington an exciting place to begin and build a career.

Where to Live

Before climbing through the ranks on the political scene, newcomers to Washington will have to deal with several more immediate considerations.

The first and most important will be where to live. The Washington region offers a wide variety of housing options, from urban to suburban to exurban. The range of possibilities is underscored by the fact that newcomers to the Washington area can choose among three separate jurisdictions: the District of Columbia, Virginia, and Maryland.

City Living

The District of Columbia provides several housing options for those who prefer urban environments. Those without cars (or who don't like to drive) will also find the District's easy access to public transportation, local food marts and retail stores, bars and restaurants, and other diversions preferable to suburban living. The rental market within the District of Columbia offers mostly apartment living, but it is possible to find houses available for lease in certain neighborhoods. While crime is often cited as a concern with living within the District boundaries, it is best to research the particular neighborhood of interest. It is imperative to talk with people in the neighborhood, the local police, and other resources in order to determine your comfort level with the neighborhood. In many cases, those interested in city living will find that the crime is not as bad as it is made out to be. However, crime is and should be a consideration.

Capitol Hill: The area surrounding the Capitol Building is a popular destination for those new to the city. Capitol Hill contains a variety of options, including small apartment buildings, English basement apartments (usually a separate unit beneath a privately-owned single family home), and group houses. It is home to many Members of Congress and Senators, who reside there while Congress is in session, staff members, and lobbyists. For those working on or near Capitol Hill, a short walk to the office is one of the prime benefits. Rents vary greatly depending on how close the apartment is to the Capitol and on the condition of the building. Average rents are typically $900 to $1,200 for a one-bedroom apartment.

Georgetown: Georgetown is an historic neighborhood that encompasses the area in the vicinity of Georgetown University. The neighborhood provides a mix of small apartment buildings, group houses and English basement apartments. Georgetown can exhibit a bit of a split personality: It is the address of choice for many of Washington's most prominent denizens, including Senator Hillary Rodham Clinton and former Secretary of State Madeleine Albright; it is also home to many college students who, along with revelers from all over the region, flock to the bars along M street. It is also worth noting that Georgetown does not have a Metro station within its confines, so those without cars will have to rely on buses, bikes, or foot power to get around. Average rents are steep in the heart of Georgetown; expect to pay $1,300+ for a one bedroom.

Dupont Circle: This neighborhood offers high-priced living options adjacent to the downtown area. It is home to a large gay population. Housing options include midrise apartment buildings, converted townhouses, and group

Visit Vault at **www.vault.com** for insider company profiles, expert advice, career message boards, expert resume reviews, the Vault Job Board and more.

VAULT CAREER LIBRARY

9

houses. There a large number of upscale dining and drinking establishments within Dupont Circle, with many casual spots as well. For those desiring upscale urban living with all the amenities, including a Metro station, close at hand and are willing to pay for it, Dupont Circle deserves a serious look. Average rents can approach New York City levels; one bedrooms go for $1,500+.

Adams Morgan: A funky, yuppified neighborhood located above Dupont Circle. It offers a range of city living options. Adams Morgan is home to a variety of ethnic restaurants and drinking establishments catering to just about every taste, and is viewed – by some – as Washington's version of a New York City nightlife district. There is no Metro in the immediate neighborhood, but the Woodly Park station is a short walk away. Average rents vary with location, but on average one bedrooms near the heart of Adams Morgan run $1,200+.

Cleveland Park and Northwest Washington: The area along Connecticut Avenue above Dupont Circle (as well as the Cathedral neighborhood along Wisconsin Avenue and many other similar neighborhoods in Northwest DC) offers many medium to large apartment buildings, converted townhouses, and group houses. The area provides all the benefits of city living, but in a quieter setting than Dupont Circle or Adams Morgan. Many of the housing options in this area are within walking distance to a Metro station, as well as bars, restaurants, and shops. Rents start around $1,100+ for one bedrooms.

Virginia

The neighborhoods of Northern Virginia provide housing options that range from quiet suburban to post-grad cool to quaintly historical. While it is impossible to cover all the neighborhood options, the following are among the most popular with new arrivals to the DC area. Additionally, those considering Virginia should be aware that getting around Northern Virginia requires a lot of highway driving. Those without a car will want to look at the North Arlington neighborhoods that are well serviced by the Metro System.

North Arlington: The area that stretches from along the Orange Line of the Metro through North Arlington County (from the Rosslyn to the Ballston station) is popular with recent college graduates and affluent, young families. It provides urban community living at a suburban address. The rental market tends toward medium to large apartment buildings, mostly modern but with a fair number of older "garden style" apartments still available. There is a wide range of restaurants in the area, including a concentration of ethnic eateries by the Clarendon metro station. The area is well served by public transportation and provides easy access to Downtown DC and Capitol Hill. Average rents vary, but newer buildings will charge $1,200+ for a one-bedroom apartment.

Old Town, Alexandria: The Old Town area of Alexandria County offers a mix of historic homes with a large number of restaurants, bars, and retail shopping options. The rental market consists of small to medium apartment buildings and group houses. Rentals within the historic area tend to be expensive, but better values can be found the further removed from the historic and business center. There is a Metro at one end of the Old Town neighborhood, but many rental options are a good walk from the station. One bedrooms in the historic area are pricey. Expect to pay more than $1,400 per month for a one bedroom.

Shirlington: The Shirlington area of Arlington provides good value at a closed in address. There is no metro in the area, so those interested in Shirlington should have a car (though the area is well serviced by bus routes, which connect with the Metro for those working downtown). Housing options center on garden style apartments and modern mid- and high-rise buildings. There are a few restaurants and retail establishments scattered throughout the neighborhood, but it is not a hotbed of nightlife. In all, a quiet, convenient suburban neighborhood. Rents for one-bedroom apartments average approximately $900.

Maryland

Living in Maryland provides the advantages of suburban living without having to traverse the superhighway system of Northern Virginia. Although taxes are higher in Maryland, many prefer its sophisticated dining options and easy access to the District of Columbia to Virginia.

Bethesda: The Bethesda area of Maryland is a popular location for young professionals who partake in the lively nightlife and restaurant scene. Upscale shopping is located within Bethesda and nearby. There are many different types of apartments available as well as group houses. Bethesda combines the advantages of urban living with a suburban location. There is a Metro stop in Bethesda, which combined with the large number of restaurants and bars, makes it a very walkable neighborhood in which to live. Average rents tend to be high, averaging around $1,400 for a one-bedroom apartment.

Visit Vault at **www.vault.com** for insider company profiles, expert advice, career message boards, expert resume reviews, the Vault Job Board and more.

VAULT CAREER LIBRARY   11

Takoma Park: Takoma Park defines liberal, suburban living. The municipality of Takoma Park declared itself a "nuclear free zone" in the 1980s. This neighborhood is adjacent to Northwest Washington. It has a good selection of restaurants, cafes, and shops. It provides a good mix of city living and suburban convenience in Maryland, but is less pricey than the Bethesda area. Housing options include small apartment buildings and single family homes. Average rents for a one-bedroom apartment fall around $1,000.

Silver Spring: For a more suburban lifestyle in Maryland, yet still fairly close to the city, many newcomers to the Washington area choose to settle in Silver Spring. A short drive from DC, Silver Spring offers more affordable housing than Bethesda does, but without the upscale nightlife and shopping. Housing options include many large apartment buildings. Silver Spring is serviced by *The Washington* area metro system. Average rents for a one bedroom are around $1,000

Quirks of DC Housing

Temporary housing

Since Washington is such a transient area, temporary housing is available throughout the city. Much of the temporary housing in the region caters to students interning either over the summer or during the academic year. Summer interns can often find housing through one of the area's universities. At all times, it may be possible to find a sublet by checking the classified ads of *Roll Call* or *The Hill* (the two newspapers that specifically cover Capitol Hill), the *Washington City Paper*, or the *Washington Post*. Many large apartment complexes offer leases of less than one year (usually at higher prices than full-year leases). Additionally, since Washington is home to many students and visiting professionals, they should also check with Internet sublet services that post sublets available for rent (usually during the summer). Interns should also check with their employers – they can often provide additional help in locating housing.

Shared apartments and group houses

Since Washington area rentals tend to be expensive and salaries are often low, apartment shares and group houses are a very popular living option, especially for those new to the city. The benefits are a lower monthly rent check, (usually) a nicer place than many individuals could afford alone, and potentially a new network of friends. The downsides, however, are very apparent: lack of privacy and the chance that your new roommate or roommates are completely nuts. Still, there are ways to minimize the risk. By asking around, it is often possible to find an opening in a house or apartment with friends of friends. The newspapers covering the Hill, *Roll Call* and *The Hill*, have classified listings of shares offered by Hill staffers, and there are several roommate services that attempt to match people by lifestyle preference (and sometimes offer a money back guarantee). The *Washington Post* and *The Washington City Paper* classifieds also include listings of shares and group houses.

How to Locate Housing

There are a number of ways to search for housing in and around Washington, many of which can be accessed via the Internet or by placing a call. Since housing options are so diverse, your search will be easier if you narrow down your neighborhood preferences in advance. Also, knowing what type of housing you are looking for will also help reduce the search time.

The following are all good sources for locating housing:

The Washington Post: *The Post* has an extensive listing of apartments for rents and roommates wanted classifieds. The Saturday edition has the most listings, with the Sunday and the Friday editions also good bets. www.washingtonpost.com

Washington City Paper: Washington's alternative weekly is a good source for housing and roommates, particularly within the District of Columbia, but suburban listings are also included. The *Washington City Paper* publishes on Thursdays and is available at coffee shops, bars, restaurants and in newspaper boxes all over the city. www.washingtoncitypaper.com

Roll Call: One of the papers that covers Capitol Hill, *Roll Call* has a classified section that includes both rentals and apartment shares. It publishes three days a week, and is accessible online at www.rollcall.com

The Hill: Another paper that covers Capitol Hill, it publishes on Wednesdays and includes classifieds for rentals and shares. www.thehill.com

Congressional bulletin boards: For those in Washington, the bulletin boards outside the House and Senate cafeterias are good sources of potential housing options. People with a place to rent or a room to fill often hang advertisements for the vacancies. Bulletin boards are located across from the cafeterias in the Longworth, Rayburn, and Cannon House Office Buildings and the Hart, Dirksen, and Russell Senate Office Buildings.

Real estate agencies: Many real estate agencies maintain listings of apartments available for rent. They are worth a call, particularly if you know the area you want to live in, and can find an office in that neighborhood.

Apartment services: There are many apartment services that match renters with apartment communities in the DC area. They are particularly helpful in locating rentals in the large complexes that pay for their services.

Roommate finders: There is a small cottage industry in Washington of referral services that match roommates. For a small fee, these roommate finders will put an apartment seeker in touch with a variety of folks looking for a new roommate, and will screen for preferences (such as smoking or gender). They can be a good source for those new to the city who would prefer to find a group house or share an apartment.

Sublet.com: A source for short-term housing in the Washington, DC area as well as other major cities.

Inside Capitol Hill

Capitol Hill is the heart of politics in Washington, DC, and for many newcomers to the nation's capital, it will be their first stop on a career in government and politics. For some, Capitol Hill will be a brief stay; for others, their experiences will carry on throughout their careers. It is not unusual for Capitol Hill staffers to leave the Hill and come back in another capacity or for a different Member of Congress. In the end, the experiences can be very rewarding. There is a small coterie of Congressional staffers who wield as much power as some Members of Congress. And for those who chose to move on after several years, the next step is often a lucrative position with a government relations firm, lobbying shop, or public affairs agency.

The Basics of Capitol Hill

As most U.S. students know from high school civics class, the U.S. Congress is divided into two houses, the House of Representatives and the Senate. Both legislative bodies meet in the Capitol Building, and are given similar powers by the United States Constitution. Chief among those powers is the power to pass legislation, which must be approved by a majority vote in both bodies, and signed by the President, to become law. Or, if the president vetoes the legislation, a two-thirds vote of both houses is required for the measure to become law.

The U.S. House, which is the lower body of Congress, is comprised of 435 Members from across the country each representing a district of approximately 647,000 people, according to 2000 census data. Members of the House stand for election every two years. To be elected to the U.S. House of Representatives, an individual must be at least 25 years old and must have been a citizen of the United States for at least seven years.

The Senate, the upper chamber, is comprised of 100 Senators – two from each state regardless of the state's population. Senators serve six-year terms, with one-third of the seats up every Federal election year. In theory, the Senate has greater stability in its Membership since only one-third of the seats are contested in any given election year. To serve in the U.S. Senate, individuals must be at least 30 years old and must have been a U.S. citizen for at least nine years.

While a majority vote of both houses is required to pass legislation, the House and Senate have several distinct powers. The House has sole power to initiate

Visit Vault at **www.vault.com** for insider company profiles, expert advice, career message boards, expert resume reviews, the Vault Job Board and more.

VAULT CAREER LIBRARY

15

legislation related to taxes. The Senate is responsible for ratifying foreign treaties (with a two-thirds vote of the body required) and confirming presidential nominees for cabinet positions, judicial vacancies, and ambassadorships.

Both the House and Senate are organized into Committees to manage the legislative process. Committees in the House and Senate have similar functions: considering and amending legislation prior to introduction on the House or Senate floor, holding hearings on legislative topics and other issues, and performing oversight of the executive branch of government.

The Republicans and Democrats in the House and Senate elect leadership teams to craft their agenda, manage the legislation on the House and Senate Floor, count votes, and communicate their messages. These elected leaders hold powerful positions in Congress that carry substantial responsibilities and create a high level of visibility for these Members.

There are a variety of sources to learn all about Congress, from its history to its workings. The web sites created by Congress contain a wide range of information on the history, structure, and workings of both Houses. The best online sources include:

- The U.S. Congress Site, www.congress.gov

- The U.S. House Site, www.house.gov

- The U.S. Senate Site, www.senate.gov

- C-Span's site, www.c-span.org, contains a helpful primer and Q&A section on Congress

- Thomas, the legislative information site of the Library of Congress: Thomas.loc.gov

Life on Capitol Hill

What is life like on Capitol Hill? In a word: fast.

Behind the headlines on any given day in the nation's capital there are a thousand sub-plots taking form: the Member of Congress and her staff working at breakneck pace to prepare a bill to reform Federal education programs; a last minute compromise to pass a key piece of legislation; a House Member positioning himself for a run for even higher office; a reporter about to break a big story about a new scandal. The environment is continually changing, and the confluence of national politics, local interests, ambitions, and personal agendas creates a sense of constant flux and excitement.

In any position on Capitol Hill, an employee's first responsibility is ultimately to serve the interests of his Member (and his or her constituents). And all of the 535 total Members of Congress have very distinct interests. Some love the national spotlight, and spend what seems to be a majority of their time before a news camera (or in search of one). Others are masters of the legislative process and use their position to propose and advance legislation. Many style themselves as hometown heroes who keep a low profile and focus on directing Federal benefits to their districts.

Despite their style, certain elements mentioned above will be true of all Members of Congress: All will attempt to direct Federal resources to their districts and attend to their constituents needs; all will use the media to communicate their messages and build (or repair) their images; and all will be involved in the legislative process to some degree, either as legislative technicians, advocates, or simply as voters.

Each Member of Congress also has his or her own distinct management style. The organization of a Member's office greatly reflects the individual personality and goals of the Member. Some offices are very formal, requiring business attire at all times, while others are less traditional. Some Members are very hands-on in running their offices, while others delegate much of the decision-making to their senior staff. Some have track records of keeping loyal staff, while others turn over staff on a championship pace. All of these factors – and many more – contribute to the pace of life on Capitol Hill.

Why Capitol Hill?

If you ask Hill staffers why they choose to work on Capitol Hill, you will get a number of different answers. Most, however, will express some common themes: They want to work on issues that they believe in; they want the opportunity to serve their country; and they enjoy using the skills needed to succeed on the Hill and pace of life it requires.

"One of the most exciting aspects of working on the Hill is the opportunity to participate in the workings of our democracy," says one Senate staffer. "The prestige of the place is nice, but for me the real satisfaction comes from knowing that the work we do makes a difference in the lives of real people."

Visit Vault at **www.vault.com** for insider company profiles, expert advice, career message boards, expert resume reviews, the Vault Job Board and more.

VAULT CAREER LIBRARY

17

A former House staffer stresses the opportunity to work on a variety of issues as one of the prime benefits of working for Congress. "I can't think of anywhere else where you can work on so many different issues in the course of the day. It's perfect for people who are curious about a lot of things and enjoy the intellectual challenge of understanding multiple issues and putting that knowledge to use on a day-to-day basis."

Another staffer, while acknowledging the benefits of working for Congress, says that the lifestyle will not be for everyone. "Things move very fast on the Hill. If you can't keep up, or you can't – for lack of a better term – multitask, you will probably not be happy here in the long run. This is a place for high energy people who get charged up from going into work every day not knowing exactly what to expect."

Working on the Hill can provide unique experiences that very few other positions afford, including international travel, the opportunity to work with national media, and the opportunity to be involved in shaping history.

"One of the greatest experiences was seeing a piece of legislation that my boss was active in passing signed into law," relates one staffer. "Looking back on that bill today, it is clear that it has helped small businesses to grow and provide good jobs for a lot of people in our district and across the country."

The opportunity for travel, both domestically and internationally, is also cited as a benefit of working on the Hill, particularly for higher-level staffers. "Many organizations sponsor fact finding trips both here in the United States and abroad," says one staffer. "These travel opportunities allowed me to gain a better understanding on a lot of key issues."

Considering working on the Hill?

If your considering working on the Hill, you should make sure you know what you're getting into. Here, we give you a quick self-assessment test to see if a career on Capitol Hill seems like a good fit for you.

The Hill is probably for you if

- You like excitement and the idea that every day can bring something different.

- You enjoy following public affairs and reading the newspaper.

- You like talking about politics...a lot.

- You don't mind starting off paying your dues by answering the phone, writing letters, and taking calls from angry constituents.

- You don't care what your work space looks like, so long as you have a desk and a computer.

- You work well under pressure.

The Hill is probably not for you if

- You'd rather be doing anything other than talking about politics.

- You prefer stable, predictable environments.

- You don't like talking to random people during the course of your day.

- You want the security of a distinct career path.

- You don't like long, unpredictable hours.

Organization of Congressional Offices

While Members of Congress are given wide latitude in organizing their office staffs, there is a typical structure to Representatives and Senators' offices. Office staffs are divided between several offices in Washington and in the Member's home district or state. Members of Congress keep most of their staffs in their Washington, DC offices. Washington is where all the legislative work takes place, and where the Member performs many of his or her official duties. Depending on the size of the district or state each Members serves, he or she also maintains one or more district offices. The district offices assist constituents with matters relating to the Federal government, such as locating lost Social Security checks or helping a small business understand the Federal procurement process.

House offices

According to the Congressional Research Service (CRS), the average House Member's office employs 14 people – on average eight in the Washington office and six in the district offices. Some Representatives will have more – others will have less. However, a "typical" structure for a Member's office will look something like this:

Visit Vault at **www.vault.com** for insider company profiles, expert advice, career message boards, expert resume reviews, the Vault Job Board and more.

VAULT CAREER LIBRARY   1 9

Washington, DC offices

Chief of staff/administrative assistant: The top aide to a Member of Congress, the CoS/AA manages the daily operations of the office, attends to the Member's needs, and is usually responsible for personnel decisions. The chief of staff is directly answerable to the Member and must maintain the trust of his or her boss. The chief of staff will sometimes work – strictly on his or her personal time – attending to the political needs of the Member, such as fundraising and campaign organization. (In some offices, this position is based in the district office to keep management closer to the people the Member represents. However, in most cases, the CoS/AA is based in Washington since the Member spends most of his or her working time there and the bulk of the staff is there).

Legislative director: With responsibility for all legislative matters, the legislative director must have mastery of the legislative process and be familiar with a variety of issues, particularly those issues most important to the Member. The legislative director will typically oversee a small staff of legislative assistants/correspondents. The legislative director is the point person on all legislative matters, including introducing amendments, tracking legislation in committee, and advising the Member on how to vote on specific bills/amendments. Another key responsibility of the legislative director is overseeing the Member's correspondence with constituents.

Communications director/press secretary: Playing a distinct role in the Member's office, the communications director or press secretary is responsible for ensuring that the Member's constituents (i.e. the voters) are aware of the work that the Member is doing on their behalf. The communications director writes press releases, schedules media interviews for the Member, briefs the media on the activities of the Member, and designs periodic updates on the accomplishments of the Member that are mailed to constituents. The communications director must be skilled at understanding both complex legislative and political issues and communicating the Member's accomplishments in a manner that creates a positive "identity" for the Member. In that sense, a communications director is often considered a political strategist (along with the chief of staff/AA) to the Member.

Legislative assistants: A Member's office will often hire several legislative assistants, or LAs as they are commonly called, (two to four LAs is the norm) to assist on legislative matters. Each legislative assistant will be assigned issues for which he or she is responsible. A legislative assistant's responsibilities include tracking legislation and issues relevant to his or her assigned areas; responding to constituent inquiries on those issues, drafting correspondence for the Member, and advising the Member on votes.

Legislative assistants must be familiar with the legislative process, and will often meet with constituents and professional lobbyists to discuss the Member's positions on issues before Congress.

Legislative correspondents: A House Member will often hire one to two Legislative correspondents (or LCs), who function as junior legislative assistants. LCs are often given issues to cover, but their primary responsibility is to draft correspondence to constituents on those issues. Occasionally, LCs will be given a few issues to manage as legislative assistants would.

Scheduler/office manager: Often this is a combined position, while at other times there are two individuals hired for these separate functions. The scheduler manages the Member's busy schedule, and often has responsibility for accepting and declining invitations, setting aside time for meetings with constituents, lobbyists, and staff, and keeping track of the Member's whereabouts at any given time. The office manager is responsible for ensuring that office bills are paid, that administrative matters are attended to, that the supply cabinet is filled, and that the office runs smoothly.

Systems administrator: Washington offices usually have one person responsible for the computer systems (including both hardware and software). This is a key position in that this person is responsible for the software that manages the Member's correspondence. The systems administrator is responsible for working with vendors to fulfill this software requirement and assisting the staff in implementing the software and generating reports on the efficiency of the Member's mail operation. Often this position has combined responsibilities, such as with a legislative assistant or legislative correspondent position.

Staff assistant: The entry-level position in a Member's office, the staff assistant is typically responsible for front desk operations, taking requests from constituents for flags flown over the U.S. Capitol, arranging tours of the White House and the Capitol Building for constituents, and a range of administrative tasks. Often, staff assistants will be given the opportunity to learn about the legislative process and other office functions in preparation for a promotion within the office hierarchy.

District offices

District director: The district director typically oversees the operations of the district offices, including district casework, personnel decisions at the district level, and constituent relations. The district director will often "stand in" for the Member at district events that he or she cannot attend. Many House

Visit Vault at **www.vault.com** for insider company profiles, expert advice, career message boards, expert resume reviews, the Vault Job Board and more

VAULT CAREER LIBRARY　21

Members have more than one district office, depending on the geographic size of their districts. Those representing large areas (entire states in some cases) will have several principal offices and additional satellite offices that are open by appointment only.

Caseworker: A Member will often have several caseworkers in the district (and occasionally one caseworker in the Washington office, as well). Anywhere from two to five caseworkers would be considered typical of a Congressional office. Caseworkers assist constituents in their dealings with the Federal government. Their responsibilities can include tracking down lost Social Security checks, assisting veterans in collecting their benefits, and expediting passport applications, among many others.

Staff assistant: District offices usually have one or two staff assistants who help staff the reception area and assist the other office staff.

Senate offices

Not surprisingly, Senate offices typically employ many more staffers than do House offices. Senate offices have greater variability in the number of staffers employed, since individual office budgets are determined by population of each Senator's state. The average size of a Senate office staff is 35, with approximately 23 staffers in the Washington office and 12 in the district offices.

Senate offices tend to be organized along the same lines as House offices (with some exceptions):

Chief of staff/administrative assistant: As in the House, a Senate chief of staff/AA is responsible for managing office operations, attending to the Senators needs, and making personnel decisions. Since in a Senate office there are more staff and a larger constituency than there is in a House office, the chief of staff may chose to delegate some responsibilities to a deputy.

Deputy chief of staff: Works underneath the chief of staff to ensure that staff functions are being properly carried out, that work is being completed as assigned, and that budget is properly managed. Reports to the chief of staff/AA and takes on special projects at the direction of the Senator and the chief of staff.

Legislative director: Directs the legislative activity of the Senator and manages a staff of legislative assistants and legislative correspondents.

Legislative assistants: Since a Senate office typically employs more legislative assistants than a House office does, Senate LAs usually have fewer issue areas but more freedom to explore their issues in depth.

Legislative correspondents: Senate offices typically hire more legislative correspondents, who respond to constituent inquiries and work closely with the legislative assistants to develop the appropriate responses.

Communications director: Many Senate offices have an entire communications department overseen by a communications director, who is responsible for the Senators' image in Washington, DC and in the Senator's home state. Since there are fewer Senators, and it is considered a more prestigious position than the House, Senator's press operations are more likely to deal with the national press, in addition to local press, on a regular basis.

Press secretary: Many Senate offices, particularly in larger states, hire a press secretary to work underneath the communications director. Often, the communications director and the press secretary split media responsibilities, with the communications director handling national media and major in-state media such as the large market daily newspapers and televisions stations, and the press secretary dealing with smaller dailies, small market television, and radio stations.

Speechwriter: Many Senate offices hire a speechwriter who is responsible for producing floor statements, speeches to national and local organizations, and media statements. Senate speechwriters sometimes split their time between another function within the office, such as legislative assistant or press secretary.

Communications assistant: Unlike House offices, many Senate offices hire a communications assistant to help the communications director and press secretary. The communications assistant typically has administrative and logistical responsibilities, such as maintaining media lists, distributing news releases, and coordinating media appearances for the Senator.

Staff assistant: Senate offices employ several staff assistants to handle front desk operations, assist constituents, and perform administrative tasks.

Visit Vault at **www.vault.com** for insider company profiles, expert advice, career message boards, expert resume reviews, the Vault Job Board and more.

VAULT CAREER LIBRARY   23

Where to Work: House or Senate?

To an outsider, the House and Senate may seem fairly similar: both are national legislative bodies; both meet in the U.S. Capitol Building; both represent prestigious offices. To the insider, however, the House and Senate embody different values and traditions.

The House is chaotic. Like a very large family around the dinner table, the 435 Members of the U.S. House of Representatives are clamoring for attention at the same time they try to grab a piece of the action for their district and themselves. Leading the House of Representatives has been likened to "herding cats." The House is also where ideas percolate freely, and where new members spread their legislative and political wings. House offices tend to be cozy, close knit organizations that often operate as much like families as professional workplaces. The House has a younger, less solemn attitude than does the Senate. It was designed by the authors of the U.S. Constitution to be closer to the people, and that goal is reflected in the two-year terms and the greater number of members as compared with the Senate.

The Senate exudes prestige. The nation's 100 Senators take pride in their Chamber's reputation for senatorial courtesy, even while they vigorously compete to advance their agendas (or derail their opponents'). Because it can take 60 votes in the Senate to bring a bill to the floor for a final up or down vote, the Senate rules encourage compromise and give legs to the Minority Party's demands. Senate offices are larger, and more bureaucratic. The Senate was designed by the country's founders to go more slowly and deliberately than the House of Representatives.

Some longtime Capitol Hill staffers identify themselves only as Senate or House people. The truth is that a position in either body can be a great stepping stone to a long and prestigious career in Washington. Where one's preferences lie will depend on his or her personality and experiences. The House has proven to be valuable training camp for the Senate – both for Members looking to step up to the higher body and for staffers wanting to assume greater visibility and authority.

GETTING HIRED

Visit Vault at **www.vault.com** for insider company profiles, expert advice,
career message boards, expert resume reviews, the Vault Job Board and more.

VAULT CAREER LIBRARY   25

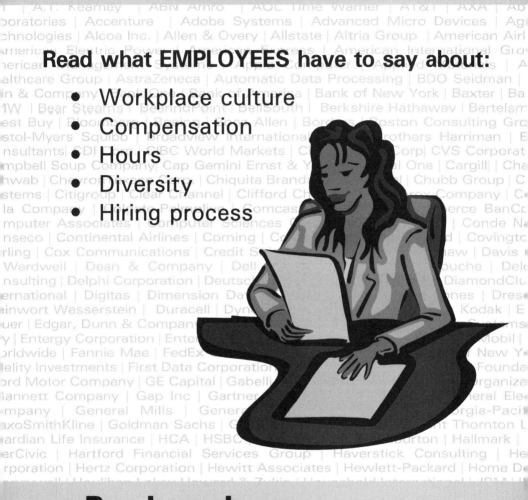

Internships in DC

CHAPTER 4

For undergraduates interested in government, politics, or specific causes, Washington, DC offers perhaps the best opportunity to gain experience and develop a rewarding career. Undergrads will have access to a wide range of opportunities in government, public affairs, and politics, since these professions require a constant source of new recruits who are eager to help advance their agendas. With experience, undergraduates will often find that rapid career progression is possible, and that they will have plenty of opportunity to assume high profile positions.

There are a host of options for undergraduates looking for their first job in Washington, DC's political scene. There is more than one way to break into the political world, and it is very common for individuals to move from one area to another. The following are some of the more common sources of positions for recent graduates.

Capitol Hill: Positions on Capitol Hill are traditionally viewed as starting points for recent graduates. New Congressional staff members usually start at low pay, but gain the experience and contacts necessary to assume higher level legislative, communications, and political positions.

Political parties and interest groups: Advocates abound in Washington and provide a wide range of career opportunities. Political parties, labor unions, nonprofits, and interest groups all offer starting points for undergraduates in areas including, grassroots organizing, issue advocacy, and legislative research, among others.

Government relations/public affairs: Trade associations, lobbyists, and public relations agencies offer a large number of entry-level as well as advanced positions that often pay better than other opportunities.

Think tanks: Many undergraduate (as well as graduate) students will be interested in research positions within Washington's many think tanks. These can provide an opportunity to work with leading scholars and contribute to Washington's knowledge industry.

Internships – The Best Way to Break In

The best way to begin a career in Washington, DC is to begin the job search before graduation by gaining experience and making the right contacts. While there will be some who possess impressive political connections

Visit Vault at **www.vault.com** for insider company profiles, expert advice, career message boards, expert resume reviews, the Vault Job Board and more.

VAULT CAREER LIBRARY   27

without having set foot in Washington, most people don't live next door to a U.S. Senator or attended private school with the White House Chief of Staff's daughter. For those without such privileges, Washington internships are the usual and best route to networking and gaining on-the-job experience.

There are two keys to opening the door to a Washington, DC career: who you know and what you know, or put even simpler, contacts and experience. An internship is a valuable way to gain both. Undergraduates with a strong desire for a career in Washington should heed one piece of advice: intern early and often.

Every summer, the nation's capitol is flooded with interns from across the country. They come from colleges and universities, graduate schools, law schools, and even a few with their degrees already in hand. Some see an internship as a good way to spend the summer. Those with stronger ambitions and real passion for what they are doing will use the summer internship to launch their careers.

There is no shortage of internships in Washington. However, it must be noted that many internships are not paid, and many more receive only a modest stipend. Additionally, competition for the most coveted positions is often intense.

Steps to finding the right internship

1) **Identify your interests early.** There are so many possibilities to choose from, it is very helpful to narrow your focus to a few areas to focus on. Some questions you will need to answer: are you a Republican or Democrat? Are you more interested in advocacy or the nuts and bolts of the legislative process? Is there a specific issue or cause you would like to support, or would you prefer a more general introduction to the workings of Washington?

2) **Make contacts.** In securing an internship, often the best resource is someone who can directly pass along your resume or put in a good word for you. Be creative in your search. Professors, friends from school, parents' acquaintances, and even neighbors can all help turn up leads. Alumni are a good source, and many will be happy to talk about internship opportunities with their employers. Additionally, many universities run internship programs for credit. Information on these programs is usually available at the campus career resource center.

3) **Get application requirements.** Applying for internships can feel a little like applying to college. Many organizations will require a current resume, a copy of your college transcript or GPA, an application form, personal references, personal essays, and/or an interview. Furthermore, many internships have application deadlines well in advance of their start dates. Even if they don't have specific deadlines (and many members of Congress don't) it is worth contacting offices and organizations up to six months before you plan to intern to determine the requirements and ensure that your application is considered in a timely manner.

4) **Prepare your applications.** Applications can take time, and potential interns are urged to clear some space on their busy schedules to prepare their applications, particularly if an interview or essays are required. In other words, start early! Essays are very common on intern applications. One Congressman asks for a one page essay on "the role you think the federal government should play in the daily lives of Americans." Another asks what you hope to achieve through your internship. The best answers show an understanding of the Member's positions and philosophy while at the same time demonstrating your personal interest in government. Essays should be kept to the required number of words or pages and clearly and thoughtfully articulate your position or goals.

5) **Choose your internship carefully.** It is not uncommon for a student to have more than one internship offer. Students should evaluate their offers carefully, taking into account the level of responsibility they will receive, their long-term interests, compensation, and the potential contacts that can be made. Additionally, it is important to decline internship offers in a timely and professional manner. After all, they may someday have to work with these organizations or even want to work for them!

Potential Interns – Know Thyself

With so many potential choices, the question often becomes, where should one apply for internships? For many undergraduates, a little research will go a long way to finding an answer.

First and foremost, undergraduates must really consider their political leanings. Washington, DC is a very partisan town, and the wrong internship can often times close doors rather than open them. The most basic question an undergraduate should consider is, what is his or her party affiliation? If you are not sure, don't take this question lightly. Your internship can "brand" you in the eyes of a future interviewer.

At the same time that the nation is becoming less overtly partisan – especially as the percentage of voters registering as independent or unaffiliated with the two major parties continues to grow – Washington maintains its sharp partisanship, and in many ways has become more deeply divided along party lines over the last decade.

This trend has some real implications when it comes to choosing internships. Crossing party lines is difficult, and can have a negative effect. Consider the example of a political science major who leans toward the Democrat Party, but whose principal interest is the legislative process. His professor can help him get a coveted legislative internship with his home state Republican Senator. Should he take it? Only he can answer that question, but he should be aware that his decision could impact his future career. He could very well land a position with a Democrat employer in the future, but he will certainly have some explaining to do. Politics demands loyalty, and even one transgression will be viewed suspiciously. Two or more is very difficult to explain, and most employers will never give you the chance.

For those who want to play it safe, or who do not necessarily feel strongly about either party, there are several options for "non-partisan" internship, including:

Trade associations: Many Washington trade associations – for example industry groups representing doctors, realtors, the car industry – operate in a non-partisan environment since they must lobby both parties of Congress. Although some have stronger partisan leanings (think small business vs. unions), most are focused on a set of industry issues that are neither Republican nor Democrat.

Government relations and public affairs firms: Many lobbying shops and public relations agencies hire folks from both parties. They are driven to serve the needs of their clients and therefore hire both Democrats and Republicans to represent their issues before Congress or the media.

The media: Most media outlets consider themselves neutral territory (although some outsiders disagree). For those with a background or interest in journalism, the many Washington media outlets offer a good source of internships.

Capitol Hill Internships

Some of the most powerful people in Washington have never run for office, yet they command as much power as many of Members of Congress. And many of them began their careers answering phones or writing letters as interns on Capitol Hill.

Traditionally seen as the starting point to a career in government and politics, Capitol Hill offices are flooded with resumes every year from undergraduates eager to gain experience and contacts to begin their ascent to Washington power broker. Internships are available in the personal offices of Members of Congress – both Senators and Representatives. Additionally, Committees on both the House and Senate side offer internships.

"Interning is the best way to get your foot in the door," said one former intern who used the experience to find a full time position. "The minute I walked in on the first day of my internship, I knew that I wanted to work on Capitol Hill. The office was buzzing with activity, the televisions were tuned to the House floor, and everyone in the office was young and dedicated. Interning allows you to experience the excitement of Capitol Hill and build the skills and contacts you will need to start a career."

There are two important considerations to make in applying for internships on Capitol Hill: where you want to work and what you want to do. Most of the internships offered by Congress will be with Members' personal offices. The Congressional committees and House and Senate leadership offices all offer internship opportunities as well. The following descriptions provide some of the differences and advantages of each type of internship. Please read the subsequent sections on Capitol Hill to gain more in-depth understanding of Congressional offices and the range of activities employees do in each on a day-to-day basis.

Personal offices

Personal offices of both Senators and Members of the U.S. House of Representatives reflect the individual personality and management style of the Members. Representatives' Washington, DC offices usually have 8-10 employees. Senators' Washington offices are much larger in terms of employees and the staff sizes are based on the population of the state each Senator represents. (Please see the next section for information on typical DC offices).

Visit Vault at **www.vault.com** for insider company profiles, expert advice, career message boards, expert resume reviews, the Vault Job Board and more.

VAULT CAREER LIBRARY   31

In general, House offices will feel more intimate (some might say cramped) than the Senate offices. In the House, interns generally work on a variety of topics, depending where the staff feels their skills can be best utilized. Due to their larger staffs, Senate offices may be able to provide a greater degree of specialization in an area of interest to the intern, such as the legislative process or media relations. Despite these differences, much of the experience will be the same regardless whether one chooses the House or Senate; answering the phone, responding to constituent inquiries, processing requests for flags flown over the U.S. Capitol, and helping visitors are all part and parcel of the intern experience.

In applying for internships, students should definitely consider the Members of Congress that represent their home towns and their college's or university's location. To find information on a Member of Congress, including an internship application, visit the Member's personal web site. Web sites for House Members can be accessed at www.house.gov and Senators sites can be found at www.senate.gov.

Committees

The Committees of the U.S. Congress offer internships. The Committees are where much of the legislative process takes place. Internships with a committee provide the opportunity to learn about specific areas of legislation (e.g. tax policy or the annual appropriations process) and to dig deeper into the legislative process than a similar internship in a Member's personal office. Since Committee staffs do not answer to constituents as Members' staffs do, interns will spend much less time writing letters. However, they most likely will not get the same level of interaction with a Member of Congress and the senior staff as interns do in a personal office.

Leadership offices

The Republican and Democrat members of the House and Senate elect leaders to organize their parties, set their agendas, count votes, and communicate their messages. The top elected leaders in each party are given separate offices and staffs to carry out their responsibilities. These leadership offices are another source of Capitol Hill internships for students. Since there are fewer leadership offices and staff members, and since members of the leadership enjoy high profile positions, internships with these offices will be very competitive.

Outside the Washington Beltway

While most students focus on internships inside the Beltway, there are opportunities where they live and study to build experience and make contacts. One of the best ways to become involved in the process is to volunteer for a political campaign. Closely contested Senate and House races require an army of unpaid labor to help achieve a victory on Election Day. Volunteers will often have the opportunity to work closely with the candidate and his or her top campaign staff. Moreover, a victory by their candidate provides a ready-made path to an internship or position on Capitol Hill. Contacting the appropriate local or national party committees can help turn up races that need assistance.

Additionally, many Members of Congress offer internships in their district offices. While the work focuses more on constituent aid than on the legislative process, the schedule may be more flexible to accommodate school hours and the experience could provide entry into the Washington, DC office after graduation.

When to intern

The busiest time in Washington for interns is during the summer. The streets of Washington literally seem to be teeming with undergraduates. Summer internships provide a good opportunity to network with other interns and enjoy a wide range of social activities. Furthermore, Congress tends to be very busy during the early summer months of June and July. Congress takes an August recess during Washington's hottest month, and the pace of life slows down greatly on the Hill and across the city. Internships at times other than the summer can be a very good option since there will be fewer interns and more work to go around. Often, they are combined with college programs for credit. However, students should work to ensure that Congress is in session while they are in Washington; interning during November and December of an election year will greatly reduce the value of the experience since Congress rarely has any official activities scheduled during this time.

Visit Vault at **www.vault.com** for insider company profiles, expert advice, career message boards, expert resume reviews, the Vault Job Board and more.

VAULT CAREER LIBRARY 33

The White House and the Executive Branch Internships

The White House and agencies of the Executive Branch offer numerous internship opportunities for undergraduates. White House internships are very prestigious and extremely selective; interested candidates should put significant time and effort into completing the required application.

Interns at the White House perform a variety of office and support functions while learning how the White House and the executive branch of government work. One of the biggest perks of the White House internship is the opportunity to serve alongside some of the best-known names in government and politics, and even meet the President or Vice President of the United States.

Internships with the White House provide access to White House events and ceremonies, a "speaker series" and a sendoff with the President. Interns report work that ranges from clerical (answering the phone, editing publications) to involved (helping to plan a Rose Garden ceremony), but that is always exciting due to the location and prestige of the internship. "Walking into the White House every day is perk enough," said one intern, expressing the truly unique experience.

There are specific requirements for applying for a White House internship: Applicants must be at least 18 years old, and they must be citizens of the United States. Furthermore, applicants are required to receive security clearance and sign a consent form to be subject to random drug tests.

Internships are available within a large number of White House offices, including the Communications Office, Office of Counsel to the President, Legislative Affairs, Political Affairs, and the Office of Presidential Correspondence. It is worth noting that White House internships are not paid; therefore applicants should plan in advance to save money or work a part time job if necessary.

Information on the White House internship program and the internship application form can be found at www.whitehouse.gov/government/wh-intern.html.

Political Parties

Those with a taste for political combat or a strong partisan streak should consider internships with the official Republican or Democratic Party committees. Internships are usually available in functions such as communications, opposition research, political field work, and fundraising. Party committees will accept more interns in national election years (even numbered years when the entire House of Representatives and one-third of the Senate is up for election, and in particular, Presidential election years, which occur at four year intervals).

The Democratic National Committee and the Republican National Committee are located within two blocks of the U.S. Capitol; both run extensive internship programs. In addition, each party maintains separate committees focused specifically on races for the U.S. House and the U.S. Senate: The National Republican Congressional Committee (NRCC) and the Democrat Congressional Campaign Committee (DCCC) offer internships focused on races for the U.S. House of Representatives, while the National Republican Senatorial Committee (NRSC) and the National Democratic Senatorial Committee (NDSC) offer internships focused on U.S. Senate races.

Advocacy Organizations

For students more interested in a cause than a specific political agenda, or for those students who want to broaden their Washington, DC experience beyond Capitol Hill, nearly every organization and every cause is represented in some form or another within the nation's capital. Many of these are large organizations that provide internships for students. However, please be aware that internships will vary from organization to organization: some will be well structured, others less so; many will offer pay or stipends, but many more will not; some will be smaller organizations while others will be larger and more bureaucratic. It is imperative for students to do their research.

While the list of advocates within Washington is too numerous to cover in great detail, there are many organizations on the right, left, and even in the center that students may wish to explore.

For example, students interested in the issue of gun control could apply for internships on either side of the debate, depending on their philosophy, and still work with some of the most influential organizations in Washington. The National Rifle Association and the Brady Campaign to Prevent Gun Violence both offer legislative internships in their Washington area headquarters.

Students interested in environmental issues should consider the liberal-leaning World Wildlife Federation or Sierra Club, while those who favor a conservative philosophy on the environment could look into opportunities

Visit Vault at **www.vault.com** for insider company profiles, expert advice, career message boards, expert resume reviews, the Vault Job Board and more.

VAULT CAREER LIBRARY

35

with a think tank or the Council of Environmental Republican Advocacy or a business organization.

There are many organizations that are also non-partisan, and that represent a professional group or other point of view. For example, the American Medical Association represents the interests of doctors before Congress and works closely with members of both parties.

Please note that it is very common for organizations with distinct agendas on both the left and the right to describe themselves as "non-partisan." While this is true in a legal sense, the fact is that many of these organizations do favor the left or the right in their activities. Students who aren't sure about an organization's true nature should cast a critical eye on its issue advocacy efforts, board of directors, and web site to determine its true leanings.

For a comprehensive list of advocacy organizations in Washington, as well as White House and Congressional staff, corporate offices and trade associations, check out the *Capitol Source*, which is published by the National Journal Group. It is available in Washington area bookstores and can be ordered on-line at www.njdc.com/about/capitolsource.

Examples of advocacy organizations

While many advocacy organizations are legally non-partisan, their politics can be considered different shades of liberal, conservative, or middle of the road. Below are some examples of various types of advocacy organizations and their ideological leanings.

American Heart Association: While headquartered in Dallas, the American Heart Association, like many medical groups, maintains an advocacy office in Washington, DC to lobby for greater research funding and promote legislation that encourages healthy lifestyles, such as anti-tobacco measures. It is considered a moderate organization. www.americanheart.org

AARP: The nation's leading seniors organization is also one of the most influential advocates in the nation's capital, making its presence felt on a number of high profile issues, including Social Security, Medicare, and healthcare issues. It is generally considered a moderate organization. www.aarp.org

Brady Campaign to Prevent Gun Violence: The Brady Campaign, named after the former White House press secretary wounded during the attempted assassination of President Ronald Reagan, works to enact gun control laws and regulation through grassroots organization and campaign support to similar-minded candidates. It is considered a liberal organization. www.bradycampaign.org

Citizens for a Sound Economy: CSE fights for lower taxes, less government, and fewer regulations. It recruits and trains grassroots activists across the country to influence the economic agenda on the national, state and local levels. It is considered a conservative organization. www.cse.org

Christian Coalition: The Christian Coalition supports policies on the federal, state, and local levels that reflect its moral values. Examples include opposition to abortion and gambling and support for lower taxes, among many social and economic issues. It is considered a conservative organization. www.cc.org

Concord Coalition: The Concord Coalition advocates for fiscal responsibility while ensuring Social Security, Medicare, and Medicaid remain secure. It was founded by the late former Senator Paul Tsongas (D-MA) and former Senator Warren Rudman (R-NH) and is considered a moderate organization. www.concordcoaltion.org

National Resources Defense Council: The NRDC supports environmental protections and engages in advocacy on issues ranging from global warming to nuclear waste. It is considered a liberal organization. www.nrdc.org

National Rifle Association: The National Rifle Association provides an array of services to gun owners and is a well known legislative advocate in the nation's capital. The NRA opposes legislation that regulates gun ownership and supports candidates that agree with its positions on gun issues. It is considered a conservative organization. www.nra.org

Common Cause: Common Cause is a strong proponent of campaign finance reform and actively lobbies to reduce the amount of money in the political process. It is considered a liberal organization. www.commoncause.org

Think Tanks

One of the most important currencies of Washington – the strength of ideas – is often formed in think tanks. In general, think tanks study issues and policies, issue research reports, hold conferences, and work with elected officials to turn their ideas into reality.

These idea generators are fueled by in-house scholars and research fellows. An intern with one of these organizations will often have the opportunity to assist in research (along with performing administrative duties) and

Visit Vault at **www.vault.com** for insider company profiles, expert advice, career message boards, expert resume reviews, the Vault Job Board and more.

VAULT CAREER LIBRARY   37

participate in forums and other activities sponsored by the think tank. Internships with a think tank can expose students to some of the leading scholars on a variety of policy topics, from international relations to tax policy.

As with most of Washington, DC, the think tanks fall along ideological lines, but the divisions are more subtle than the sharp fault lines of national politics. For example, within what would generally be described as conservative think tanks, there are major players representing conservatives (Heritage Foundation), libertarians (Cato Institute) and neo-conservatives (American Enterprise Institute). On the liberal side, major players include the Brookings Institute and the Center for International Policy.

Beyond the most prominent think tanks, there are many others organized around a single issue or idea. For example, the Foundation for the Defense of Democracies was formed to address solutions to international terrorism in the wake of the September 11 attacks.

Many think tanks offer internship programs, and the specifics of the experience will vary greatly among the many programs. However, in general, students should look for a few key attributes in researching internship opportunities with think tanks:

- Does the think tank's philosophy match your own? If not, it could lead to an unhappy experience among people who by their very nature are *very* opinionated.

- Will the internship provide a range of experiences and contacts, or will the experience be limited (i.e. spending 90 percent of your time answering phones)?

- Will there be an opportunity to be involved in the research or publication of the organization's scholarship?

Examples of think tanks

The American Enterprise Institution: A conservative-oriented think tank, AEI researches and promotes a strong national defense, limited government and private enterprise. www.aei.org

The Brookings Institution: A more liberal-oriented think tank, the Brookings Institution offers policy solutions to a variety of issues, including economics, government reform, and international relations. www.brookings.org

The Cato Institute: Libertarian in orientation, the Cato Institute supports public policies that strengthen individual liberty, free markets, limited government, and peace. www.cato.org

The Center for International Policy: Focusing on a liberal approach to foreign policy, the Center for International Policy promotes a U.S. foreign policy based on international cooperation, demilitarization, and respect for human rights. www.ciponline.org

The Heritage Foundation: Founded in 1873, the Heritage Foundation formulates and promotes conservative public policies based on free enterprise, individual freedom, a strong national defense, traditional American values, and limited government. www.heritage.org

Progressive Policy Institute: The Progressive Policy Institute serves as a think tank for moderate Democrats and promotes foreign policy, economics issues, and government reform that reflects a less liberal approach than traditional Democrat views. www.ppionline.org

Government Relations/Public Affairs

Trade associations, government relations firms, and public relations agencies often run internship programs focused on the legislative process, policy development, and issue advocacy. While not as prestigious at the Hill internships, experience in these areas will help build Washington know-how, develop contacts, and provide an understanding of the role of the private sector in the legislative and policy-making process.

For clarification, government relations refers in general to the lobbying done by corporations, trade associations, advocacy organizations and lobbying and law firms. Lobbying involves developing positions on issues before Congress and advocating for the passage or defeat of specific legislation. Public Affairs refers to the process of communicating with various constituencies through the media, public speaking opportunities, and issue advertisements. Corporations, trade associations, advocacy groups, and public relations firms all engage in public affairs activities either on behalf of their own issues or on behalf of clients (in the case of the P.R. agencies).

Finding an internship in this area will require some research. Students should use their network of contacts and consider areas that they are interested in. For example, students interested in environmental policy may want to explore internships with law firms that do a lot of lobbying on the issue.

Visit Vault at **www.vault.com** for insider company profiles, expert advice, career message boards, expert resume reviews, the Vault Job Board and more.

VAULT CAREER LIBRARY   **39**

Another good reason to examine internships in this area is that the senior staffs of lobbying firms and P.R. agencies in Washington were often former high-level staffers with Congress or the executive branch. Therefore, interns can gain experience at the feet of some of the most respected practitioners in their fields.

Duties with lobbying firms or legislative affairs offices of trade associations typically revolve around research and attending Congressional hearings and other public events to gather information, writing issue summaries, and administrative tasks to assist the senior lobbyists. Interns at public relations firms will learn how to write press releases, organize media events, and design media relations strategies.

Organizations Sponsoring Internships

Many people can find internships through educational programs run through institutions of higher learning or private organizations. These programs combine classroom learning with internship experience and usually provide college credit to participants. Be aware that many of these programs require students to pay for educational expenses and lodging, and do not provide a stipend for the internship. Typically, these programs are only open to current students, and therefore not appropriate for career changers.

Since many colleges and universities run their own internship programs, students should check with their schools about internship opportunities. Additional providers of internships include:

The Washington Center: The Washington Center runs a program that combines academic credit with internship placements in government, political organizations, the media, business, lobbying, public affairs, and advocacy groups, among many others. Students apply directly to the Washington Center, and it helps arrange for internships. The Washington Center provides several benefits: class one night per week; a wide range of internship options with organizations that work closely with the Washington Center; a Program Supervisor is assigned to each participant to serve as a guide in selecting internships and making the most of the program; access to housing; and scheduled lecture series and other academic and social events. The Washington Center places approximately 1,000 interns a year and has a relationship with more than 800 colleges and universities. However, potential participants should note that there is a cost associated with attending the Washington Center. The cost is determined by many factors, including financial assistance, so those interested in applying should begin to explore the process early and the range of options available to them. For the Summer Term 2003, programs costs are $3,420 and housing costs are $2,925.

Fund for American Studies: The Fund for American Studies, in partnership with Georgetown University, sponsors both semester and summer programs that combine internships with learning and networking opportunities. Both programs offer internship placement, housing, and courses for credit. The semester program runs from September through December of 2003. During the summer, the Fund offers three separate institutes focused on: politics and economics, journalism, and business and government affairs. The Fund for American Studies promotes an understanding of free markets and limited government. The Fund for American Studies charges tuition for its services; the total program cost for Spring 2003 was listed as $8,950 plus expenses. The summer programs, of which there are three, total $4,780 for 2003 including program and housing costs. It offers need-based scholarships (approximately 60 percent of students receive assistance). Interested students should contact the Fund for complete information, including application requirements and the details of the various programs. The fund can be found on the Web at www.dcinternships.org.

Visit Vault at **www.vault.com** for insider company profiles, expert advice, career message boards, expert resume reviews, the Vault Job Board and more.

VAULT CAREER LIBRARY   41

Identifying Opportunities and Standing Out

CHAPTER 5

Capitol Hill is the epicenter of political life in Washington. A job on the Hill is usually seen as the starting point for a career in politics and government in Washington. Someone coming out of an undergraduate program with a passion for either should seriously consider starting on the Hill.

Finding the first position on Capitol Hill is a function of two factors: contacts and experience. The good news for job seekers is that both can be developed very quickly in Washington's hyperactive atmosphere. The bad news is that positions are still very competitive and a job search will usually take some time. Still, those with a passion to work on the Hill and a strong willingness to be persistent should be able to find something in due order.

As mentioned earlier, the best way to gain experience and contacts – and thus to get your foot in the door – is through one or more internships during school or immediately following graduation. The benefits of interning are measurable and immense:

- **Internships can lead directly to employment.** Interning with a Member of Congress can lead to an offer of full time employment. Many Members' offices give first consideration to their current or previous interns when an entry-level opening occurs. Internships allow you to directly access the decision makers within the office and help you to create advocates for your candidacy among the staff.

- **Internships provide references.** Even if your internship doesn't lead directly to a job offer – and that can be the case simply because the Member's Office or organization simply doesn't have an opening – most sponsors of interns will be happy to write a letter of recommendation or make a call to a potential employer on an intern's behalf.

- **Internships develop experience.** Many employers will want to see evidence of your experience in government or politics. While a thesis on the role of the media in the legislative process is impressive, even more important are concrete examples of a work product, such as constituent letters or a press release. An internship will allow you to prove to future employers that you are capable of doing the real, and very practical, government work .

Visit Vault at **www.vault.com** for insider company profiles, expert advice, career message boards, expert resume reviews, the Vault Job Board and more.

VAULT CAREER LIBRARY   43

However, if you haven't had a chance to do an internship before graduation but suddenly have your heart set on a career in government and politics, don't despair. There are as many ways to get your foot in the door as there are lobbyists in the nation's capital.

First, for those who have just graduated and even for career changers, consider moving to Washington. It is very difficult to search from outside of the DC metropolitan area, and it is very rare for a Washington employer to pay transportation and lodging expenses for an entry-level job interview.

Second, consider doing an internship. If you are a recent college graduate, and don't mind working a second job to support yourself, it's not too late to find an internship while you look for a full-time position. Many organizations and Members of Congress will offer internships to recent college grads. While these internships will most likely pay little, if at all, they provide the same benefits noted above. And moreover, they provide a solid base to conduct an extensive job search.

Third, don't discount the power of networking outside of work. There are people who landed their first jobs on Capitol Hill because they tended bar at their future boss' favorite watering hole. Washington offers literally hundreds of networking opportunities, from organized softball leagues to cultural organizations to active school alumni clubs. On any given night in the nation's capital, there is no shortage of possible venues that can lead to the contacts necessary to finding that first job. Washington lives and breathes politics every day, and that doesn't change on weekends or when the sun goes down.

Fourth, if it is campaign season, volunteer to work on a campaign. Winning campaigns tend to bring a lot of their staff to work in Washington. And even losing efforts will expose you to many new contacts, including party officials, consultants, and other campaign staff members.

Identifying Opportunities

Getting a job with a Member of the House of Representatives or a Senator can be difficult. There is a limited supply of positions and there are always many applicants, sometimes hundreds, for each opening.

Assuming your internship or campaign stint didn't land you one of those positions, how do you go about finding openings? The best method is to throw a wide net:

Networking: Most positions on the Hill are never advertised; instead, they are filled through word of mouth or personal references. It is not unusual for Members offices to begin receiving resumes even before a staff departure has been made official. Word spreads very quickly around the Hill of new vacancies, so having your ear to the ground is often the only way to hear about them. Creating a personal network is the best way to get access to these openings. A strong network serves several purposes:

- It will help you learn about new opportunities.

- Your network will serve as references.

- People in your network will often know the decision maker in the office; if they think highly of you, they can make a proactive call to sell your candidacy.

Beyond your network there are several more ways to identify potential opportunities:

- **Start with your hometown Representative and Senators.** Members of Congress generally prefer to hire people from their own districts or states. Therefore, it is always good to stop by and introduce yourself to the Representatives that represent your region and your state's two Senators (of course, only visit those of the same party). They are much more likely to take a serious look at your resume, and staff members may be willing to offer extra assistance to your job search.

- **Search help wanted listings.** The two newspapers of Capitol Hill, *Roll Call* and *The Hill*, run employment sections that often contain advertisements from Members of Congress and Committees seeking to fill positions. These advertisements generate loads of responses, but at least it is certain that the Member is looking and that your resume will at least be screened for potential employment. Another extensive source of positions is the bi-weekly publication, *Opportunities in Public Affairs*, which lists many openings on and off Capitol Hill (and is available in many bookstores or online at www.opajobs.com).

- **Keep on top of Capitol Hill job banks.** The U.S. House and Senate offer separate resources for job seekers: The Senate Employment Bulletin can be accessed via phone at (202) 228-5627 or in the Senate placement office. The listings are updated every Friday. The House of Representatives Jobline is (202) 225-2450 (press 4-2). Additionally, following every election the Committee on House Administration provides a resume drop

Visit Vault at **www.vault.com** for insider company profiles, expert advice, career message boards, expert resume reviews, the Vault Job Board and more.

V/\ULT CAREER LIBRARY   **45**

area where anyone can submit their resume to be distributed to the newly-elected House Members.

- *Pound the pavement.* While it is not very efficient, many people have landed their first positions by dropping resumes off with every Member of Congress they are interested in working for and hoping for the best. Some choose to focus on a small number of Members based on geography or ideological interests, while others use their cover letters to stress their interest in specific issues the Member is working on. While a job seeker can either mail or e-mail in their resume, often dropping off the resume in person can be the most effective, since it will give you a chance to talk to the receptionist to learn if there are any positions open and to get the name of the appropriate person to follow up with.

- **Look for experience with a retiring Member:** One way to gain temporary experience and to get a paycheck at the same time is to accept a position with a retiring Member of Congress. Much of the staff for retiring Members will begin their job searches well before the Member leaves office in the hopes of transitioning to their next position without having to go through a period of unemployment. For the unemployed job seeker, especially those without much previous experience, taking a position with a retiring Member is a good way to build a Capitol Hill resume. Sure, the position will end soon, but it can beat interning.

- **Work on a campaign.** It can't be stressed enough that campaign work is a very good way to find a job in Washington. Winning congressional candidates tend to bring their campaign staffs with them to Washington, DC. Even if campaign work doesn't lead to a position, it is a great way to network and build a reputation within the political world.

- **Think about professional associations and other affiliations.** Many people have affiliations that they can tap into that will help their job searches. For example, consider family and friends that belong to professional associations. If one of your parents is a realtor and is active with the National Association of Realtors, then the Washington office of the association might be able to help you network and identify opportunities.

Sample Resume

Jane Bagley
123 Fourth Street, S.E.
Washington, DC 20003
(202) 555-5555

EDUCATION

UNIVERSITY OF NOTRE DAME, Notre Dame, Indiana
Bachelor of Arts in History, 2002
GPA: 3.5/4.0
Received Academic Honors all four years
Served as admissions volunteer

WORK EXPERIENCE

DEMOCRATIC NATIONAL COMMITTEE, Washington, DC
Research Assistant, 7/2002-12/2002
• Wrote research reports for use by national, state, and local candidates on a variety of issues, including tax policy, national security, and education.
• Worked with key campaign staff to develop messages to be used against Republican opponents.
• Supported the press office by providing timely research and information about Federal policies and Congressional votes.

JANE SMITH FOR STATE LEGISLATURE,
Volunteer, Fall 2001
• Assisted on a part time basis with a campaign for the state legislature.
• Staffed the campaign office and greeted visitors, providing them with information on Smith and her stands on the issues.
• Led a team delivering campaign literature door to door. Determined routes and organized volunteers.

ST. JOSEPH'S MEDICAL CENTER, South Bend, Indiana
Internship, Spring Semester 2000
• Assisted with office functions, including scheduling patients, organizing patient files, and maintaining inventory of office supplies.
• Utilized Microsoft Excel to track office expenses.

OTHER

• Fluent in Spanish; conversational French.
• Proficient with Microsoft Word, Excel, and Powerpoint.
• Member, Democratic Party of Indiana.

Visit Vault at **www.vault.com** for insider company profiles, expert advice, career message boards, expert resume reviews, the Vault Job Board and more.

VAULT CAREER LIBRARY   47

Sample Cover Letter

Dear [Chief of Staff or whoever is responsible for employment decisions]:

I am writing to apply for a position as a staff assistant for Congressman John Doe. While growing up in Nebraska's 7th District, I greatly admired Congressman Doe's efforts to improve the local economy and serve as a strong voice for social welfare programs. It would be an honor to work for Congressman Doe to help him fulfill his agenda in Washington.

During the 2002 campaign, I served as a research assistant with the Democratic National Committee, a position which ended following the campaign. While at the DNC, I supported many state and national campaigns by preparing extensive research reports and writing issue summaries for candidates and campaign staff. Additionally, I assisted a successful state legislative campaign during my senior year at the University of Notre Dame. I helped staff the campaign office and greeted visitors who wanted information on the candidate. I also coordinated several literature drops around the district, and was an active participant in the campaign's phone banks.

Through my experiences, I have developed strong organizational skills that will allow me to contribute to your office operations. During my tenure at the Democratic National Committee, I took on responsibility for coordinating all the research reports that were being sent out to candidates to ensure that they were delivered in a timely manner. Before I assumed the project, requests for information were being passed from senior staff members to research assistants who then were responsible for sending them out. Unfortunately, since there were so many requests, some were never actually making it to the campaigns. I set up a system to track the requests and then check-off when they had been delivered. The system is still being used now.

This is a very exciting opportunity. I am certain that I would be a good representative for Rep. Doe and would be able to contribute to the office in a very positive way.

Thank you for your consideration. I will follow up with you next week to schedule a time to meet.

Sincerely,

Jane Bagley

Networking

Without question, networking and the ability to foster long-term relationships are at the heart of any successful career in Washington. It begins with your first position and continues throughout your time in the political community, whether it is on the Hill or in a related profession such as lobbying or public relations.

"Without a doubt, networking is the most important part of any job search," says one long time Hill staffer, now a lobbyist. "When I was looking to fill a position, I would always be receptive to candidates referred from people who I trusted. We would get a lot of unsolicited resumes, but unless they really stood out for some reason, they would rarely land an interview."

Another Hill staffer advises people interested in working on the Hill to get to know as many people on the Hill as possible, through both social and professional networks. "Washington, DC really is a small town when you come down to it. The people that work on the Hill and in politics are a small, insular community. For those new to town, it is important to get to know as many people up here as possible. Definitely do an internship, get involved in outside activities, go to parties with other Hill staffers, and try to get to know as many people as you can."

For those conducting a job search, especially first time job seekers new to the city, establishing a network can be challenging. There are several good ways to begin to build a network, including:

- **Request informational interviews.** Meet with as many people as possible who work in organizations related to what interests you. Many people are receptive to helping newcomers to Washington and providing career advice. Contact people in your home state congressional delegation and others identified through friends, family, professors, and previous experiences. Not everyone will have the time or inclination to meet with you, but there will certainly be some that will. Most people in Washington began their careers much like you are now, so they remember what it was like to find that first position and will be open to helping out.

- **Join staff organizations:** There are many staff organizations on Capitol Hill, some of which are open to non-Hill staffers. Join all of those that interest you, and get involved with the clubs when you have time. Some examples include the Congressional Legislative Staff Association, Republican Communications Association, the Lesbian and Gay Congressional Staff Association, Congressional Black Associates, and

Visit Vault at www.vault.com for insider company profiles, expert advice, career message boards, expert resume reviews, the Vault Job Board and more

VAULT CAREER LIBRARY   49

many others. A list of staff organizations and contacts can be found at the Committee on House Administration web site, www.house.gov/cha.

- **Get involved in activities you enjoy.** Washington offers tons of opportunities for people to get involved in things that they enjoy, which also provides for networking opportunities. For example, there are many softball leagues in and around D.C., including an active league pitting Capitol Hill offices against one another. There are many charitable activities organized by Hill staff and other young Washington types. One could also become a junior member at one of the small art galleries, which host receptions and educational opportunities, such as the Corcoran Gallery of Art or the Phillips Collection.

- **Volunteer for political activities.** There are always elections taking place within D.C. or in the metro area. Get involved with local political parties or look out for opportunities to help out the national parties on races.

How to Stand Out

With so many applicants, it becomes imperative that candidates stand out in their cover letters and resumes, and later in their interviews. While each candidate brings his or her own unique abilities to each application, there are several universal assets to consider in applying for Capitol Hill positions:

- **Demonstrate strong writing abilities.** Positions on Capitol Hill, particularly at the lower levels, often require candidates with strong writing skills. Legislative correspondents and legislative assistants will spend much of their time writing letters: to constituents; to interest groups; to other Members of Congress; to the President; and even some letters that are meant more for the media than for the addressees. They often are responsible for drafting the floor statements of their bosses. Those interested in media relations will need to be able to write press releases, speeches, opinion editorials, and newsletters. Therefore, it is important that candidates present resumes and cover letters that are grammatically correct and that effectively communicate their abilities. Poor grammar and sloppy writing will serve as proxies for the candidate's ability to write and his or her attention to detail. You don't need to be John Updike, but you will need to show an above-average command of the English language. In your resume and cover letter, stress your ability to write and reference examples of your work. In fact, you should include a short writing sample with your resume, especially if you have a letter or a press release from one of your previous internships. Additionally, experience working for a school newspaper or other experience demonstrating writing ability is looked upon well.

- **Emphasize organizational and leadership skills.** Congressional offices are fast paced and require employees to juggle multiple job responsibilities. Additionally, staff members at all levels are representatives of the Member of Congress – from the staff assistant greeting visitors to the office, to the chief of staff representing the member before a community meeting, every staff member has a direct influence on the perception of the Member. Therefore, offices are looking for people who are organized, presentable, and who have strong interpersonal skills both in person and over the phone. Possible ways to demonstrate these abilities are through extracurricular activities, previous work experience, or leadership positions. Emphasize these characteristics in all application materials and be prepared to describe your accomplishments in these areas in interviews.

- **Exhibit knowledge of Member and his or her key issues.** It always helps to be able to show that you are truly interested in working for the specific Member to which you have applied. Fortunately, researching your target is very easy, since Members of Congress leave a trail of relevant and timely information on their activities, including media stories, floor statements, and voting records. Your approach to the Member of Congress should be tailored around your strengths and the interest of the Member. For example, if you grew up in the Member's district, highlight your understanding of the concerns of people there, your involvement with political, community, or civic organizations, and your support for initiatives championed by the Member. Likewise, you could also address your experience, possibly from a previous internship, on a national or local issue that your targeted Member has been active on. Members' offices are looking for people who will be effective in advancing the Member's agenda and who will be a good fit with the rest of the staff. Demonstrating some level of affinity can be very effective in your job search.

- **Show your loyalty to the cause.** Your prior political experience will be closely scrutinized when you submit your resume on Capitol Hill. Make sure to highlight internships, experiences, and volunteer work that are relevant to the Member's office to which you are applying. For example, don't include campaign work for a libertarian candidate unless you know the Member to which you are applying is sympathetic to the libertarian movement as well. In almost every case, do not highlight any experiences working for the other party unless you are prepared to explain in some depth why you should still be considered for the position. There are exceptions to this rule. For instance, someone interested in environmental

Visit Vault at **www.vault.com** for insider company profiles, expert advice, career message boards, expert resume reviews, the Vault Job Board and more.

VAULT CAREER LIBRARY   51

conservation policy would want to include their work on that issue, regardless of the party, if the member to which they were applying shares the same views (such as a Democrat staffer applying for an environmental L.A. position with a Republican member known to champion environmental causes).

Some Members and their Issues

While representatives and senators are actively involved on a wide range of issues that affect their constituents, there are certain Members that become champions of specific issues. These are the issues that they are most passionate about, and that can – for better or worse – define their careers. A small sampling of Members who have demonstrated strong leadership on specific issues are highlighted below.

Senator Chuck Schumer (D-NY): Gun control legislation has been one of the highest priorities on Senator Schumer's agenda. He first took up the issue in the U.S. House of Representatives and carried his crusade to the Senate. His major legislative initiatives include coauthoring the assault weapons ban and sponsoring the Brady Bill, which instituted background checks for handgun purchases.

Senator John Breaux (D-LA): Among the many issues Senator Breaux champions, perhaps the most high profile is his longstanding support for reforming the nation's Social Security system – the so-called third rail of American politics, since the very notion of touching Social Security can be a political death sentence. In 1998, Senator Breaux co-chaired a commission looking into Social Security reforms. He is currently working with a bi-partisan group of Senators to introduce reform legislation, and has demonstrated his willingness and ability to bridge partisan divides to strengthen Social Security.

Rep. Tom DeLay (R-TX): As the Majority Leader of the United States House of Representatives during the 107th Congress, DeLay is responsible for guiding the Republican agenda. One of the issues he champions personally and with devotion is reforming the foster care system. To advance the cause, he as reached across the aisle to partner with Senator Hillary Rodham Clinton (D-NY) to reform the way the Federal government spends some $7 billion per year to protect children from abuse, place children in foster care, and provide adoption assistance. In his personal life, he and his wife Christine have taken three foster children into their Houston home.

Senator John McCain (R-AZ): Senator and former presidential candidate John McCain's name has become synonymous with campaign finance reform. Along with co-sponsor Senator Russ Feingold (D-WI), McCain pushed through the campaign finance reform legislation that bore his name and bucked his party in the process. Today, with campaign finance reform a reality, both the Democratic and Republican parties are facing a new set of challenges in raising money and funding their candidates for Federal office.

Visit Vault at www.vault.com for insider company profiles, expert advice, career message boards, expert resume reviews, the Vault Job Board and more.

VAULT CAREER LIBRARY   53

Rep. Steve Buyer (R-IN): When he isn't attending to the needs of his constituents in rural Indiana, Rep. Buyer can be found championing the interests of military men and women from his position on the Armed Services Committee of the U.S. House of Representatives. One of his most successful causes has been securing benefits for the victims of the series of maladies referred to as "Gulf War Syndrome." Buyer served in the 1991 Gulf War as a reservist, and suffers from many of the same symptoms. As a result of his efforts, he was portrayed in the 1998 Showtime film, "Thanks of a Grateful Nation."

Rep. John Linder (R-GA): Representative Linder has led the fight to overhaul the nation's tax system. The "Fair Tax" championed by Linder would replace the income taxes, payroll taxes, Capitol gains taxes, and death taxes under the current system with a national retail sales tax. Linder believes that this change will dramatically improve the nation's economy by reducing compliance costs, cutting the costs of goods and services, and giving citizens some level of control over their taxes. Linder once again introduced his legislation to the U.S. House in 2003 as he continues to build support for it among his colleagues and across America.

Rep. Lynn Woolsey (D-CA): As a former welfare mother, Rep. Woolsey has spent much of her energy in Congress on opposing welfare reform policies that she believes hurt those most in need of assistance. Instead, Woolsey has cosponsored legislation to provide aid to the poor through stronger educational services, greater focus on job training, and increased funding for child care. As a senior Democratic member of the Committee on Education and the Workforce, Woolsey advocates for such issues as paid family leave and improving child support collection.

Sen. Joe Lieberman (D-CA): As a senator, candidate for Vice President in 2000, and a declared presidential candidate for 2004, Senator Lieberman has been a strong advocate for oversight of the entertainment industry and the effect of graphic portrayals of sex and violence on children. As Chairman of the Senate Committee on Governmental Affairs, he held hearings on video game violence and pushed game makers to adopt a rating system to warn parents about violent content. He was a cosponsor of legislation that would crack down on the marketing of hyper violent media products to children and he has joined with former Education Secretary Bill Bennett to pressure the entertainment industry to behave more responsibly.

The Interview

In many ways interviewing on Capitol Hill is like interviewing for any other position. Potential employers will want to know about an applicant's work history, accomplishments in previous positions, educational achievements, and ability to fit into the office. While qualifications are important, there are many overly qualified individuals applying for the most basic entry-level positions. Therefore, finding a position on the Hill often comes down to the question of "fit." Impressing the right people is often the key to landing a position.

For entry-level positions, applicants may be screened by a lower level staffer. Usually, however, a more senior staffer or the Member makes the final decision on hires.

With 535 Senator and Representatives' offices making hiring decisions, it is difficult to characterize a "typical" interview. Much will depend on how the individual office screens and evaluates candidates. However, don't expect to find the human resources efficiency of a private company. Offices are small, and hiring decisions are just one of the many responsibilities pressing on senior staff at any given time.

"When I interview candidates, I'm trying to get a sense of how they will perform on the job," says a staffer with hiring responsibility. "I want to see examples of relevant work experience, strong writing samples, and find out whether or not they can handle the fast pace in our office. I'll usually ask them to describe a situation where they had to juggle several responsibilities at once. I like to see campaign experience, because that shows that they can handle the intensity of politics."

One of the most common mistakes applicants interviewing for entry-level positions make is to over-tout their credentials while underwhelming the interviewer with their enthusiasm for the position. For example, an applicant who implies that his master's degree in international relations and internship with the English Parliament make him overqualified for writing constituent letters, but nonetheless he is willing to stoop to such a position in order to advance his career, is unlikely to land the job. Rather, it is important for a candidate to stay focused on the position being advertised and on demonstrating how his or her skills and dedication will assist in the office operations and allow him or her to be an asset to the Member's team.

Visit Vault at **www.vault.com** for insider company profiles, expert advice, career message boards, expert resume reviews, the Vault Job Board and more

VAULT CAREER LIBRARY 55

"Sometimes you get people that come across as too arrogant," says a Democratic staffer. "If they act that way toward me, imagine how they will treat a constituent."

Interview Advice

- **Dress professionally.** This should go without saying, but nevertheless, too many applicants arrive for the interview dressed inappropriately. In general, dress on Capitol Hill is conservative. For men, appropriate dress includes a dark suit and a shirt and tie and dress shoes. Women should wear a tastefully tailored suit of appropriate skirt length with dark dress shoes with a low heal. Both men and women should be well groomed and present themselves in a professional manner. Remember, as a staff member you will be representing your Member of Congress. Dress as you would expect to be greeted by a staff member of a Member of Congress.

- **Be prepared to answer the "Why."** Interviewers will often want to know what drives an applicant to apply for a position on Capitol Hill, particularly at the entry level. Clearly, many of the well-educated college grads who are applying could make more money elsewhere. Be prepared to talk about your interests, passions, and goals (a common interview question is to ask where you see yourself in five years).

- **Stress geographic commonalities.** Members prefer to hire candidates from their home districts or states. If you grew up in the district or the state, be sure to stress the connection. However, other connections exist and can help impress the right interviewer. Did you go to school in the district? Do you regularly visit a relative in the state? Does your family vacation there?

- **Know the Member and the district/state.** There is so much public information available about Members of Congress, there is no good excuse to show up unprepared. The best place to begin is with a Member's personal web site. House Member's web sites can be accessed at www.house.gov and Senators web sites are linked at www.senate.gov. Member's web sites will include information on the district, a biography on the Member, recent news releases, and other information on issues and accomplishments. Independent media reports also provide important background information. Another good source for basic research, particularly about the district the Member represents, is the *Almanac of American Politics* published by the National Journal Group, which is available at many bookstores in Washington or online (or save money and borrow it from a friend or find it at the library).

Sample Interview Questions

Since there is no centralized hiring process for Capitol Hill, every interview experience will be different. However, there are some familiar themes that will come up, as illustrated by the following samples questions. Provided as a guide only are some thoughts on responding to these questions.

1) Why do you want to work for [Member of Congress]?
This is a chance for the interviewee to show that she has done her research and is familiar with the Member and his record. The reasons may relate to geography (born and raised in the Member's district, know the people there); specific issues (support the Member's issues and have done relevant research/work on some of them); or ideology (believe in the cause championed by the Member of Congress).

2) You understand that this position requires a lot of administrative duties, such as answering the phones, opening the mail, and greeting visitors. How do you think you will perform these operations?
This question gets to the heart of the specific duties for the position. The interviewer knows you are smart – now she wants to see that you know what you are getting into and will actually perform the job.

3) Tell me about an activity that you were involved with in school or work that demonstrates your leadership skills and your ability to get things done.
Capitol Hill offices are fast paced and require everyone to pitch in. The interviewer is trying to gauge your ability to pick up a project and see it through to completion.

4) Are you an organized person? Show examples from your previous experience where you demonstrated your organizational skills.
Working on the Hill means that assignments are coming at you three at a time. As a staff assistant you may have two constituents on hold on the phone, a family of four standing in front of you waiting for their White House tour, and two staffers asking about projects you were assigned – all at the same time. Provide specific examples of your ability to juggle multiple responsibilities.

5) Where do you see yourself in five years? Ten years?
This is a popular question, so be sure to think it through before you go into the interview. Interviewers would like to get a sense of how serious you are as a professional and of your long-term interests. No one will ever hold you to it, so make sure that your answer makes sense.

Visit Vault at **www.vault.com** for insider company profiles, expert advice, career message boards, expert resume reviews, the Vault Job Board and more.

VAULT CAREER LIBRARY   57

6) What is one of your weaknesses?

A popular question in any setting. There are lots of interviewing advice books that have lots of suggestions on how to answer this one. Be honest, but don't be too self-critical about your abilities to handle some of the key functions of the position (i.e. if you are applying for a staff assistant position, don't ever reveal that you are disorganized. Think of another one.)

7) What are your strengths?

Stress those strengths that will make you a good fit for the position you are applying for, not just the ones of which you are most proud.

The Offer

Getting an offer on the Hill can be difficult work. The perfect resume and great connections are no guarantee of employment. For most, especially, those new to Washington, getting an offer will take some time. Whether it takes a day or three months, many Hill veterans recommend that you accept any offer you receive rather than holding out for a better position to come along. Once you get your foot in the door, there will be plenty of opportunities to explore different positions and other offices. "Take the offer and run with it," said one political staffer with a party organization. "You can always move on to something else if it doesn't work out."

ON THE JOB

Visit Vault at **www.vault.com** for insider company profiles, expert advice, career message boards, expert resume reviews, the Vault Job Board and more.

VAULT CAREER LIBRARY

59

Use the Internet's
MOST TARGETED
job search tools.

Vault Job Board

Target your search by industry, function, and experience level, and find the job openings that you want.

VaultMatch Resume Database

Vault takes match-making to the next level: post your resume and customize your search by industry, function, experience and more. We'll match job listings with your interests and criteria and e-mail them directly to your inbox.

> the most trusted name in career information™

Careers on Capitol Hill

CHAPTER 7

The Staff Assistant

If you are coming out of an undergraduate program, or are a recent graduate, and want to start your career on the Hill, your first position will most likely be as a staff assistant (or possibly as a legislative correspondent).

The staff assistant role is viewed as the traditional entry-level position for those with little to no Capitol Hill or legislative experience. It is not glamorous, and the pay is low, but it does provide the first important entrée to Capitol Hill.

The primary responsibilities of the staff assistant tend more toward administrative work. On the surface, a staff assistant is often seen as a glorified, college educated receptionist. As a staff assistant, you will usually be the first person a visitor sees upon entering the office. Your responsibilities include greeting guests, arranging tours of the Capitol, opening and sorting the mail, and answering the phone.

However, as a staff assistant, you will also have the opportunity to assist the more senior staff in a variety of areas and learn the ropes on Capitol Hill. As you learn the fundamentals of your position, you will have more time to put your education to use. Staff assistants often have the chance to work with legislative assistants to research legislation and other issues, take on special projects for the chief of staff, or help the press secretary by proofreading speeches and organizing media lists.

Moreover, the position of staff assistant reinforces one of the foremost truisms of work in Washington: proximity to power is key. As a staff assistant, you will perform many mundane tasks. You will be paid far less than you could command in an entry-level position elsewhere. You will also work directly for a Member of Congress and position yourself for far more interesting jobs in the future. Therefore, newcomers to Washington are hungry for an entry-level spot on Capitol Hill. It is the proximity that provides experience and opens doors to bigger opportunities.

"Getting started on the Hill means lots of time doing stuff they didn't teach you in college, like answering the phones and spending a lot of time dealing with constituents. But I wouldn't give up this job for anything. A lot of my friends off the Hill make more money, but in the long run my time on the Hill will open a lot more doors for me down the road," says one staff assistant.

Visit Vault at www.vault.com for insider company profiles, expert advice, career message boards, expert resume reviews, the Vault Job Board and more.

VAULT CAREER LIBRARY 61

"Working as a staff assistant is both frustrating and exciting," another explains. "Frustrating because some of the work can be tedious and some of the people you deal with can be quite rude. It's exciting because our office moves so fast. The Senator is very involved on many high profile issues and is always being asked to appear on television. I've been able to meet many high profile Washington dignitaries and leaders."

A Day in the Life of a Staff Assistant

8:30 a.m.: Come in to open up the office. Since you are the first person a visitor sees upon entering the office, it is your responsibility to ensure that the reception area is neatly kept and that there are plenty of brochures about things to do in Washington, DC.

8:40 a.m.: Catch up on the latest news by reading *The Washington Post*, *Roll Call* (the newspaper of Capitol Hill), and your home town papers on-line.

9:30 a.m.: Open and sort the mail. It is amazing how many people take the time to write to their Congressman. As you read each incoming letter, you must determine which legislative assistant or legislative correspondent is responsible for answering the correspondence. Reading the mail gives you a chance to learn about the issues Congress is considering.

10:30 a.m.: Welcome a family from the Member's district visiting Washington with their three children. You have already arranged a tour of the Capitol with one of the office staff.

11:30 a.m.: Answer yet another call from a constituent expressing his opposition to a bill pending before Congress. This is the tenth call you have received today on the same topic, all before lunch. One of the interests groups must be ginning up a strong grassroots operation to defeat this bill!

12:30 p.m.: Finally, time for lunch. Find one of the interns to cover the front desk so that you can slip away for 45 minutes. Head down to the Rayburn Cafeteria with two other office mates to grab a quick bite and gossip about the latest scandal stirring in Washington.

1:15 p.m.: The bells signal the first vote of the day. Activity in the office picks up as the Member prepares to go to the floor.

2:00 p.m.: Research an issue for one of the legislative assistants. Request several documents from the Congressional Research Service (CRS).

3:30 p.m.: The strange person who claims that the CIA implanted a chip in his brain and is monitoring his thoughts calls yet again asking to speak to the Congressman. You tell him that your boss is not available, but that you will be sure to pass along the message.

4:00 p.m.: Head down to the basement of the Capitol Building to pick up flags that have been flown over the U.S. Capitol to send to constituents that have requested them. The tunnels under the Capitol are mazelike – you are always surprised when you don't get lost.

5:00 p.m.: Time to call it a day, and head out to happy hour. Members' offices are required to pay overtime to all "non-exempt" employees, including staff assistants, so unless there's something pressing, you can only work an eight-hour day.

Advancing on Capitol Hill

Advancing up the ladder on Capitol Hill begins after gaining experience in an entry-level position. Typically, a new hire as a staff assistant will work anywhere from six months to a year and a half before taking the next step (although advancement can come very quickly or not at all). Advancement often depends as much on chance as it does on talent.

There are two ways to move up on Capitol Hill: Promotion from within or finding a new position with another Member's office. Both paths offer specific benefits and pitfalls.

Advancement from within

Moving up on Capitol Hill is a function of your initiative, abilities, and rapport with the Member and the rest of the office staff. There also needs to be an appropriate opening. Often, the most frustrating barrier to advancement for the ambitious Hill staffer will be the lack of movement in the upper ranks of the office. As already discussed, Congressional offices are relatively small. In order to move up, someone above you must either move up or on. And while turnover can be high within an office, the timing will be completely out of your control. Even when an opening appears, there will be

Visit Vault at **www.vault.com** for insider company profiles, expert advice, career message boards, expert resume reviews, the Vault Job Board and more.

VAULT CAREER LIBRARY   03

no guarantee that you will be promoted to fill it. Still, in many ways, promotion from within can be the best way to advance your career on the Hill.

There are many reasons to work your way up within your Member's office. For one, most Members of Congress value loyalty in their staffs. Remaining with the same Member will allow you to build trust with your boss – a critical factor in future advancement since Members must to some degree entrust their political careers to the work of their staff members. The more the Member trusts and likes you, the greater the chances for future advancement into the senior ranks of the staff. However, it must be noted that advancement can take time. Senior staff are not created overnight. The path varies from office to office, and the variability can be quite large. In some offices, a staff member may rise from a staff assistant to be chief of staff within five years. In others, the same climb might take 10 or more.

Additionally, the longer you remain with a single Member, the greater you will benefit as that Member assumes greater responsibility. Nothing can change a staffer's position faster than her boss' advancement within the Capitol Hill hierarchy. Careers have been made by a boss' ascent to a committee chairmanship or a leadership position. The promotions arising from a Member's newfound powers are usually based on the tenure of the employ and the level of trust the staffer enjoys.

Advancement with another office

Despite the advantages of remaining with one Member during your tenure on the Hill, there are many good reasons to pursue advanced opportunities with other Member's offices.

For starters, looking for positions with other Members will give you a greater sense of control over your advancement. By applying for positions with another Member, you can test the strength of your experience and credentials on the open market, rather than waiting for an opening within your current office. You have the opportunity to sell your credentials, and can create your own career path.

Another reason to change offices is to work for a Member that more closely matches your philosophy or that you personally feel more comfortable with. As noted, offices are very small and can often feel like a family affair (particularly in the House of Representatives). Therefore, it is not unusual for staff members to feel out of step with his or her Member or to not necessarily fit with the management style of the office. For these individuals, it is natural to look at other positions outside of their current offices.

Additionally, there may be issues that you wish to cover that your current Member doesn't emphasize. If you're primary interest is transportation, it is only natural to seek out a Member who sits on the Senate or House Transportation Committee.

The Next Step – Legislative Correspondent

Typically, the next step after staff assistant or after gaining experience in a similar position with a trade association or lobbying shop is a move to legislative correspondent, either with a Senate or House Office. As noted above, this move will often come with the same Member of Congress or with another Member.

The move to legislative correspondent offers new responsibilities as well as new opportunities. In becoming a legislative correspondent, you will be free from the shackles of front desk responsibilities. While there will still be considerable administrative work – from answering the phones to logging mail – legislative correspondents have a greater opportunity to test the waters of future career paths.

In many offices, legislative correspondents are treated as junior legislative assistants. They may have a couple of low-profile issues for which they are responsible, which will allow them to build experience in the legislative process and demonstrate their ability to function as an effective staff member. Additionally, as a legislative correspondent, staffers have often had enough of a taste of the various functions to choose a track on Capitol Hill: usually the legislative track, but also the communications track or a more political track.

Visit Vault at **www.vault.com** for insider company profiles, expert advice,
career message boards, expert resume reviews, the Vault Job Board and more

VAULT CAREER LIBRARY   65

A Day in Life of a Legislative Correspondent

9:00 a.m.: Catch up on the latest national news by reading *The Hill* and scanning *The Washington Post*, *The New York Times*, and the CNN.com web site.

9:30 a.m.: Draft a form letter in response to a question on the President's proposed tax cuts.

10:00 a.m.: Log the newest stack of correspondence to arrive in the morning mail drop.

11:00 a.m.: Research issues related to proposed changes in the new education reform bill being pushed by the party's leadership.

12:00 p.m.: Three hours in the office, and you are ready for some fresh air. Slip out for a quick bite to eat from one of the many carry out restaurants on Pennsylvania Avenue.

12:45 p.m.: Make the revisions the legislative director indicated on the draft form letter you submitted for his review this morning.

1:00 p.m.: Take a call from a constituent on a small business issue. Log the constituent's name into the computer database and indicate the action taken to satisfy the constituent's inquiry

1:15 p.m.: Draft additional correspondence on behalf of the Member on a range of issues percolating before Congress.

3:00 p.m.: Attend an all-staff meeting called by the chief of staff to discuss changes in office policy to improve the response time to constituents. As a result, you must now process even more requests during the course of your busy day.

4:00 p.m.: Talk with one of the legislative assistants to get a briefing on the Member's position on changes to the Social Security system.

4:30 p.m.: Return some of the messages that have been piling up on your desk.

5:00 p.m.: Head home after yet another busy day.

The Legislative Track

Legislative assistants

Legislative correspondents interested in staying involved in the legislative side of the Hill typically build the issue experience and operational knowledge of a Congressional office to move up to a legislative assistant (LA) position. The ascent to legislative assistant can be a rapid climb or a slow one. Getting to the legislative assistant position extends your experience beyond "entry-level" and offers the opportunity to branch out in a variety of directions. But first, you must take advantage of the opportunity offered to work directly with the Member of Congress on the legislative process.

As a legislative assistant, you will become much more of an "advisor" to the Member and less of an administrative processor. Legislative assistants are given a set of issues for which they are solely responsible. They must track all legislation related to their issues, keep the Member abreast of scheduled votes on legislation under their purview, and often give advice on the best way for the Member to address pending issues. At the same time, many mundane functions will remain under their responsibility, most notably writing constituent letters. Legislative assistants on the Senate side will have fewer issues as well as fewer administrative responsibilities than their counterparts on the House side.

As an LA, you will have much greater contact with outside organizations. Often, you will be responsible for representing the Member in meetings with lobbyists, constituents, and other advocacy groups with an interest in legislation before Congress.

With additional experience, LAs will have the opportunity to assume even greater responsibility as a legislative director.

Legislative director

The role of the legislative director (LD) is very much a management position within a Member's office. LDs are typically responsible for the most important legislative activities of their Member's offices, especially legislation moving through the committees the Member sits on. LDs also oversee the work of the LAs and the LCs, and are usually responsible for ensuring the accuracy and quality of the Member's responses to constituents.

Visit Vault at **www.vault.com** for insider company profiles, expert advice, career message boards, expert resume reviews, the Vault Job Board and more.

VAULT CAREER LIBRARY   67

The traditional path to becoming a legislative director is by promotion from within a Member's office or by recruitment from outside the office, either from another Member or from a private sector employer, such as a government relations firm or an advocacy organization. In either event, most Members require that their LDs have substantial legislative experience. Additionally, LDs need to be good managers and must have a good rapport with the Member, or be able to quickly build a strong relationship.

As with other positions on the Hill, promotion to LD can take varying lengths of time, with anywhere from two to 10 years of legislative experience being the norm. The legislative director position in a Senatorial office usually requires greater experience than it does for a House office. A law degree or a master's degree in public policy can be helpful in moving up, but it is by no means a prerequisite for the position.

The Communications Track

Breaking into a communications position on the Hill – a press secretary or communications director position – can be more difficult than finding a legislative position if only because there are fewer positions overall and far fewer entry-level jobs in which to build experience. Often times, those with aspirations of becoming a communications staffer must develop their skills off the Hill.

One of the most common routes into the communications track is for a legislative assistant (or even a legislative correspondent) to be promoted to the position from within an office. Usually this person will have an expressed interest in communications and often will have some previous experience (such as having worked for his or her college newspaper) or else have solid verbal and written communications skills.

There are several opportunities to gain entry-level experience on the Hill. Senate offices often hire a press assistant to help the communications director and/or press secretary. These positions provide a good training ground to move up on the Senate side or to find a press secretary opening on the House side. Additionally, many Committees and Leadership offices hire communications assistants. In general, these positions are filled from the outside or by promoting a staff assistant or an intern with an interest in media relations.

Off the Hill, those interested in media relations should consider entry-level media relations positions public relations firms or trade associations. Entry-level positions in these areas provide the opportunity to learn the art of media

© 2003 Vault Inc.

relations, delve into public policy areas, and build a network of media and industry contacts. Since many Capitol Hill offices only make experienced hires for the communications director/press secretary positions, a few years of experience can be a very valuable tool to gain entry to a Hill position.

A third possibility is to enter directly from the media. This route has been used effectively by some, while others have found it problematic (some former reporters make fantastic press secretaries; others never quite adapt to the work on the other side of the notepad).

Regardless of how one chooses to break in, the life of a communications professional on Capitol Hill is never dull. Depending on the size of the congressional district or state a Member represents, the press secretary may deal with 20 to more than 200 media outlets ranging from small weekly papers to major daily newspapers to television affiliates.

A Day in the Life of a Communications Director/Press Secretary

8:00 a.m.: Arrive early at the office. Read all the newspapers from the district and scan the national media outlets (*The Washington Post*, *The New York Times*, *The Wall Street Journal*, CNN, *The Washington Times*, National Journal's *Congress Daily*, etc.) Compile a set of media clips from the District's newspapers for the boss to review, as well as the rest of the staff.

9:00 a.m.: Brief the boss over the phone about what's in the papers, including local coverage of Congress and national stories that appear to be "moving."

9:20 a.m.: Draft a press release on the grant your boss secured to build a new transition center for displaced workers. Layoffs have hit the District hard, and the funding will demonstrate your boss' commitment to helping her unemployed constituents prepare for jobs in the new economy.

10:00 a.m.: A reporter for the *The New York Times* calls and wants to know your boss' position on the bill to raise the minimum wage that will be voted on next week. You promise to check and get back to the reporter well before his 5 p.m. deadline.

10:30 a.m.: Take a call from a reporter from the major newspaper in the District. She wants to do a profile on the boss' efforts to loosen restrictions on adoptions. You provide background information for the

Visit Vault at **www.vault.com** for insider company profiles, expert advice, career message boards, expert resume reviews, the Vault Job Board and more.

VAULT CAREER LIBRARY 69

reporter and put together a briefing paper on the legislation and its prospects for being signed into law. You schedule a half-hour interview with the Member for a couple of days later.

11:00 a.m.: Prepare talking points for the boss for an interview with another District newspaper on the President's economic agenda.

12:00 p.m.: Lunch at your desk – again!

12:30 p.m.: Meet with the legislative director to get a better understanding of the legislation coming to the floor over the next couple of weeks.

1:00 p.m.: Breaking news – draft a response to the announcement that a major international treaty on arms control has just been ratified. Track down the boss and read the statement to her over the phone. Once it has been approved, you can get it out to make this news cycle.

2:30 p.m.: Write the script for a radio actuality the boss will record for use on local radio news broadcasts. With one recording, you can get your boss on up to 10 radio news programs. She never reads your scripts word for word, but she prefers to have them in hand before calling in her comments.

3:00 p.m.: Attend a meeting of all the press secretaries for Members in your political party. The leadership staff brief the press secretaries on the best language to use (according to the polling) in promoting the party's health care agenda.

4:00 p.m.: You return to your office to find six messages from reporters on your voice mail. Better return them pronto to see if they are on deadline and to answer their questions.

5:00 p.m.: Put the finishing touches on the speech your boss will deliver to a fundraising dinner for the party faithful tomorrow night.

6:00 p.m.: Begin drafting a press release on tomorrow's big vote on tax cuts. Since it's still not certain whether the bill will pass, you prepare preliminary drafts of two statements in either case.

7:00 p.m.: More talking points for the interview on adoption. Even though your boss knows the issue, she wants all the information on the bill available at her finger tips and in a form that can be easily communicated to the folks back home.

8:00 p.m.: Head home since tomorrow will be even busier!

The Chief of Staff

The highest ranking staff member of a congressional is the chief of staff (or administrative assistant as the position is also known). As the principal advisor to the Member of Congress, the chief of staff plays a variety of roles in the Member's office, including managing operations of the office, monitoring political developments in Washington and the home district or state, consulting with local government officials, and leading special projects for the Member.

Advancement to the chief of staff position requires strong political instincts, effective management abilities, and an ability to foster a strong sense of trust with the Member of Congress. There is no one clear cut path to a chief of staff position. Many new Members bring a trusted advisor with them to lead their offices while others hire an experienced Washington hand, perhaps a high level staffer from a Member of their home state's Congressional delegation. Established Members will often promote from within to fill vacancies while others may bring back a trusted staffer who had joined the private sector.

Given the variety of sources that Members can tap to choose their top aides, there is a high level of variability in advancing on Capitol Hill to a chief of staff position. In fact, many of the top congressional staffers never assume chief of staff responsibilities because they either don't want the administrative duties or would have to reduce their focus on their areas of expertise. However, many more staffers aspire to the chief of staff position as the capstone to their careers on Capitol Hill.

Compensation

The following are the average salaries for key Washington House and Senate staff. It is worth noting that these are averages only, and that actual pay will depend on a number of factors, including an individual's experience and the salary policies of the individual Member's office. Some Members are known to pay their staff well; others offer below average salaries across the board.

Since House and Senate salaries are published, job seekers can evaluate a Member's salary policies by examining what the Member pays his or her staff members at each level. (House salaries are published by the Chief Administrative Officer of the House in the "Statement of Disbursements of the House." Senate salaries are published by the Secretary of the Senate in the "Report of the Secretary of the Senate.") These publications are available

Visit Vault at **www.vault.com** for insider company profiles, expert advice, career message boards, expert resume reviews, the Vault Job Board and more.

VAULT CAREER LIBRARY   71

in Members' offices, so job seekers should ask a friend in a Member's office to borrow the book to research salary levels before interviewing to get a sense of the salaries they pay. They are also available at Federal Depository Libraries (locations can be found on the Web) and at the House and Senate Document Rooms.

The following table lists the average salary for the traditional office positions within both House and Senate offices.

	House	Senate
Chief of Staff/AA	$97,619	$116,573
Legislative Director	$61,075	$91,438
Communications Director	$45,301	$65,362
Legislative Assistant	$37,321	$48,276
Scheduler	$41,068	$44,273
Systems Administrator	$30,205	$39,612
Legislative Correspondent	$26,745	$25,226
Staff Assistant	$23,849	$22,504

Sources: Congressional Management Foundation (CMF), 2000 House Staff Employment Study; CMF's 1999 Senate Staff Employment Study. Both studies are cited in the Congressional Research Service's report on Congressional Member Office Operations.

Opportunities with Committees and Subcommittees

The Committees of the House and Senate carry out a large portion of the legislative process. In general, House and Senate Committees hold hearings, consider bills and resolutions (including amendments), report the bills and resolutions, and perform oversight over the executive branch.

There are two types of Committees: authorizing and appropriating. The authorizing committees have the power to enact programs, change Federal laws, and hold hearings and investigations. The appropriating committees – of which there are only two: the House Appropriations Committee and the Senate Appropriations Committee – provide the actual funding for Federal programs.

Committees typically have several subcommittees in order to make the workload more manageable. Often, legislative initiatives are first considered by subcommittees, which pass along their recommendations to the full committee. Subcommittees also hold hearings and conduct investigations.

Members of the House and Senate sit on one or more committees. Their committee assignments often determine their legislative priorities, and shape their careers in the U.S. Congress. Additionally, Members of a full committee typically sit on one or more subcommittees of that committee.

House and Senate Committees hire a substantial number of staff members for a variety of roles, including legislative, legal, communications, coalition building, and executive positions. Working for a Committee has several benefits. One, Committee staffers are able to focus on a specific legislative area, such as tax policy, health care, or education. Two, Committee staffers can dedicate most of their time to the legislative process since they do not generally work on constituent issues. Three, Committee staff positions often pave the way for future high level lobbying positions, since Committee staffers have a great deal of responsibility over their specific issue areas.

There are several ways to join Committee staffs, depending on the structure of the Committee:

- **Join as junior staff member.** Committees hire several entry-level and lower-level experienced employees for junior level roles, including staff assistants and legislative assistants. By joining as a junior level staffer, it is possible to work up to a professional staff position over time. In general, the keys to finding a position with a Committee are the same as with a Member's personal office: networking works best, but many openings are advertised in the same publications as other positions.

- **Get appointed from personal staff.** Most Committee staff members are hired by the Chairman of the Committee and the Ranking Member of the Committee. (The Chairman leads the Committee for the party holding the majority of seats in the House or Senate, while the Ranking Member leads the members of the Minority Party on the Committee.) Many new Committee Chairmen appoint members of their personal staff to assume key staff positions, such as the chief of staff and the professional legislative staff members. Subcommittee chairmen also often can assign a staff member to the Committee staff or receive separate funds to pay for a staffer assigned to the Committee.

- **Develop expertise in an issue area.** Committee staffs hire experts in policy areas, many of whom hold advanced degrees, including JDs and master's in Public Policy. Developing an area of expertise through experience on the Hill, higher education, government service, and private sector government affairs positions provide the credentials necessary for many committee slots. Often, hires from outside the committee are done

Visit Vault at **www.vault.com** for insider company profiles, expert advice, career message boards, expert resume reviews, the Vault Job Board and more.

V/\ULT CAREER LIBRARY   **73**

exclusively through networks. A senior committee staff member may approach a potential applicant he or she knows about filling the slot before the vacancy has been officially announced. One way to develop a network with Committee staffers is to work for a member on the Committee you are interested in. This will allow you to gain visibility with the Committee staff and develop an expertise on Committee issues.

House Committees

Committee on Agriculture: Oversees all legislation relating to farming programs, forestry, fisheries, and agriculture in general.

Committee on Appropriations: One of the most powerful committees in Congress, the House Appropriations committee is responsible, along with the Senate Appropriations Committee, for initiating bills spending funds of the U.S. Treasury.

Committee on Armed Services: Has jurisdiction over the Department of Defense and related national security programs in other departments.

Committee on the Budget: This committee's principal responsibility is to pass, with the Senate, a budget resolution that serves as the framework for spending decisions.

Committee on Education and the Workforce: Has jurisdiction for federal education and labor laws and some health care legislation.

Committee on Energy and Commerce: A very powerful committee with jurisdiction over issues relating to much of the U.S. economy, including telecommunications, consumer protection, food and drug safety, public health, energy, and interstate and foreign commerce.

Committee on Financial Services: Oversees the financial services industry, including the securities, insurance, banking, and housing industries. It also oversees the Federal Reserve, Department of Treasury, and the Securities and Exchange Commission.

Committee on Government Reform: Oversees Federal government activities and performs oversight and investigation into waste, fraud, and abuse in government activities.

Committee on House Administration: Has jurisdiction for legislation governing the operations of the U.S. House of Representatives.

House Permanent Select Committee on Intelligence: Oversees the intelligence budget and performs oversight of intelligence activities conducted by Federal agencies, including the CIA and the FBI.

Committee on International Relations: Oversees United States foreign policy programs and agencies and manages legislation regarding foreign policy, the U.S. Department of State, foreign assistance and many other issues.

Committee on the Judiciary: Has jurisdiction over matters related to the administration of justice in Federal courts and law enforcement agencies and oversees a range of legal issues before Congress. It also conducts impeachment proceedings against the President.

Committee on Resources: Oversees Federal legislation related to the nation's natural resources, including mining, national parks, fisheries and wildlife, and energy policies.

Committee on Rules: Responsible for setting the rules by which legislation will be considered in the U.S. House of Representatives.

Committee on Science: Has jurisdiction over all Federal non-defense scientific research and development and oversees science related agencies including NASA and the National Science Foundation.

Committee on Small Business: Oversees the Small Business Administration and has jurisdiction over many issues impacting small businesses.

Committee on Standards of Official Conduct: Also known as the Ethics Committee, it has jurisdiction over legislation regarding the official conduct of House Members and has the ability to conduct investigations and punish Members in violation of House rules.

Committee on Transportation and Infrastructure: Authorizes funding for and oversees legislation relating to highway, air, railroad, water transportation and other public works developments.

Committee on Veterans Affairs: Oversees Federal programs assisting veterans and has jurisdiction over legislation related to veterans programs and the Department of Veterans Affairs.

Committee on Ways and Means: One of the most powerful committees on the Hill, it has jurisdiction over tax policy. It also deals with other high profile issues, including economic policy, health care, international trade, and welfare.

Visit Vault at **www.vault.com** for insider company profiles, expert advice, career message boards, expert resume reviews, the Vault Job Board and more.

VAULT CAREER LIBRARY

75

Senate Committees

Committee on Agriculture, Nutrition and Forestry: Has jurisdiction over legislation relating to agriculture and forestry issues as well as some related issues, such as school nutrition programs.

Committee on Appropriations: Writes legislation that allocates Federal funds to the numerous government agencies, departments, and organizations on an annual basis.

Committee on Armed Services: Has jurisdiction over legislation related to national defense departments and programs and conducts oversight of those departments and programs.

Committee on Banking, Housing, and Urban Affairs: Has jurisdiction over legislation relating to banks and financial institutions, export and foreign trade promotion, insurance, and public and private housing.

Committee on the Budget: Responsible for drafting Congress' annual budget plan and monitoring action on the budget.

Committee on Commerce, Science, and Transportation: Has jurisdiction over a broad area of legislation, including interstate commerce, transportation, science policy, the coast guard, and sports.

Committee on Energy and Natural Resources: Responsible for legislation and oversight related to energy resources and development, nuclear energy, public lands, and mineral and water resources.

Committee on the Environment and Public Works: Has jurisdiction over legislation relating to federal environmental protections and public works projects such as highways and flood control systems.

Committee on Finance: A powerful committee with jurisdiction over a broad range of key legislation relating to taxes, international trade, the Social Security program, and health care.

Committee on Foreign Relations: Responsible for overseeing international relations policy and has jurisdiction over legislation related to U.S. foreign policy.

Committee on Governmental Affairs: Has jurisdiction over legislation affecting the efficiency and operations of government, and performs oversight and investigations of government actions and agencies.

Committee on Health, Education, Labor, and Pensions: As its name suggests, the committee holds jurisdiction over a broad range of issues, including legislation on education, labor, and health care issues.

Committee on the Judiciary: Has jurisdiction that ranges from criminal justice to anti-trust and intellectual property law. Also holds confirmation hearings for Federal judicial nominees.

Committee on Rules and Administration: Responsible for the administration of the Senate office buildings and the Senate wing of the U.S. Capitol as well as other issue relating to the operations of the Senate.

Committee on Small Business and Entrepreneurship: With jurisdiction over the Small Business Administration, the Committee uses its legislative and oversight responsibilities to strengthen the environment for small businesses and entrepreneurship.

Committee on Veterans Affairs: Exercises oversight over the Department of Veterans Affairs and has jurisdiction over legislation authorizing programs that benefit veterans.

Opportunities with the House and Senate Leadership

Members of the House and Senate Leadership also hire separate staffs for their leadership offices. Their staffs are culled from personal office staff, other Members, other leadership offices, and former Hill staffers who have left to the private sector. Leadership staff helps set the party's agenda, move the agenda through Congress, and communicate the agenda to the public.

For those with aspirations of working in a prestigious leadership staff post, there are no sure fire ways of landing such a position. Leadership staff positions are rarely advertised; rather they are filled through personal networks and by tapping experienced staff. Still, there are several ways to position oneself for a leadership position:

- **Network with leadership staffers.** Since openings aren't often advertised, it is best to keep an ear to the ground. Establishing good relationships with leadership staffers will help open doors

- **Move up with your boss.** Leaders are elected before the beginning of each Congress, and there are often significant changes due to retirement, term limits, or from challenges to standing leaders. When new Members assume leadership positions, they usually assign a number of their personal office

Visit Vault at **www.vault.com** for insider company profiles, expert advice, career message boards, expert resume reviews, the Vault Job Board and more.

VAULT CAREER LIBRARY   **77**

staff to positions in their leadership offices. Therefore, working for a Member interested in a leadership position can lead to a post, but there is no guarantee.

- **Take on leadership assignments.** The leadership often assigns Members to carry out special projects. Taking staff responsibility for a leadership project can raise your visibility and create networking opportunities.

House Leadership

Speaker of the House: The Speaker of the House is elected at the beginning of each Congress, which occurs in January of odd numbered years, by members of the U.S. House of Representatives. The Speaker of the House is the highest leadership position in the House, and is the third ranking constitutional office of the United States behind the President and the Vice President.

Majority Leader: The Majority leader is elected by the party in control of the U.S. House of Representatives to direct the floor activity of the House. The Majority leader exercises strong control over which bills are brought to the floor of the House for votes and sets the legislative calendar.

Minority Leader: The Minority Leader is responsible for the interests of the minority party in the U.S. House of Representatives. The Minority Leader effectively leads his or her party in the House of Representatives and attempts to marshal the party's efforts to present alternative legislation to that advanced by the Majority party.

Majority Whip: The Majority Whip is responsible for counting the votes on major pieces of legislation and working to ensure that the Majority Party's bills are passed by the U.S. House. The Whip often times must enforce party discipline.

Minority Whip: The Minority Whip counts votes for the member of his or her party and works to help the party vote to uphold its principles – which means often opposing the Majority Party's legislation.

Democrat Caucus Chairman: The Democrat Caucus is the official organizing body of all the Democrats in the U.S. House of Representatives and their staffs. The Democrat Caucus Chairman is responsible for developing effective messages for the party and communicating their messages to the public.

Republican Conference Chairman: The Republican Conference is the official organizing body of the Republicans in the U.S. House of Representatives and their staffs. Like his Democrat counterpart, the Conference Chairman is also responsible for message development and communications.

Republican Policy Committee Chairman: The Republican Policy Committee studies and discusses legislative proposals and the party's priorities. The Policy Committee Chairman leads the 46-member policy panel and oversees the staff.

Democrat Congressional Campaign Committee (DCCC) Chairman: The DCCC Chairman oversees the party's efforts to elect Democrats to the U.S. House of Representatives by raising funding, directing campaign operations, and leading advertising and other communications efforts.

National Republican Congressional Committee (NRCC) Chairman: The NRCC Chairman performs the same role for his or her party as the DCCC Chairman.

Senate Leadership Offices

Vice President of the United States: The Vice President of the United States serves as the presiding officer of the Senate and has the responsibility for casting the deciding vote in the event of a tie vote.

President Pro Tempore: The title of President Pro Tempore is awarded to the member of the Majority Party with the most seniority. The President Pro Tempore presides over the Senate in the absence of the Vice President and serves on the Majority Party's leadership team.

Majority Leader: The Majority Leader serves as the official leader of the Majority Party in the U.S. Senate. He or she sets the party's agenda and serves as the principal spokesperson for the party.

Minority Leader: The Minority Leader sets the agenda for his or her party and serves as the party's Senate spokesperson.

Majority Whip: The Majority Whip counts votes and works to persuade Senators to vote for their party's positions.

Minority Whip: The Minority Whip serves in the same capacity for the Minority Party.

Republican Conference Chairman/Democrat Conference Chairman: The Chairman of his or her respective party helps organize the party's activities and is responsible for communicating the party's positions and accomplishments to the American people.

Republican Policy Chairman/Democrat Policy Chairman: The Chairman of his or her respective party maintains a staff of policy experts to help shape the party's legislative policies and provide guidance to Senators for their policy development.

Off the Hill:
Political Parties, Lobbying, Advocacy

CHAPTER 8

Opportunities to be involved in government and politics in the nation's capital are not limited to Capitol Hill. In fact, there are many more jobs – both entry-level and experienced – in related positions than there are on the Hill.

For those just out of college, positions with political party organizations, with lobbying organizations, public relations agencies, and advocacy organizations can provide ways to build career experience and participate in the political process. Those so inclined can continue to apply for positions on the Hill and take extra time to build a strong Washington, DC network.

For those with Hill experience, many of these off the Hill positions, particularly in government relations and public affairs, provide an opportunity to increase their earnings and enjoy a more sane lifestyle. The decision on when to jump, and into what position, is very personal and is covered below to illustrate the types of opportunities available to people with solid Hill experience.

Political Parties and Campaign Consultants

Many of the most influential and skilled political professionals in Washington do not work on Capitol Hill. By working for a political party organization or an advocacy group, they are free to pursue their true passions with more freedom than they would have working in Congress. To be happy and effective in such an organization, however, one must truly believe in the cause it promotes.

Political Party Organizations

There are many entry-level and career track opportunities available within the national committees of the Democrat and Republican parties. During an election year, the party committees can be one of the best bets for finding an entry-level position and gaining experience and contacts (although many of the positions end immediately following the elections in November).

The party committees hire entry-level positions in their finance, research, communications, and political departments. While there will be some

Visit Vault at **www.vault.com** for insider company profiles, expert advice, career message boards, expert resume reviews, the Vault Job Board and more.

V/\ULT CAREER LIBRARY   81

differences, the committees, both Democratic and Republican, are organized along the same lines and present similar opportunities:

Research: Entry-level researchers will study the records of candidates from the opposition party and compile information that can be used against the candidates in media relations and advertising. This may include researching legislative votes, conducting LexisNexis searches of newspaper stories, and interviewing people familiar with the candidate. At the higher levels, researchers will help to build a compelling case that can be used against the candidate, much like a prosecutor might build the case against a defendant. Additionally, many researchers are responsible for specific areas of public policy and are tasked with preparing issue briefs for use by campaigns.

Political: This position is also known as Field. Entry-level political employees assist the party's candidates by playing a coordinating role between the national party and the candidate's campaign. They often serve in an administrative capacity coordinating campaign funding assistance, setting up schedules when the candidates visit Washington, or tracking polling data. At the higher levels, political professionals advise campaigns on strategy and make decisions about which races to fund with party finances. They also manage the activities of outside consultants, including advertising firms and pollsters.

Communications: At the entry-level positions, communications staffers will maintain national media lists, take messages from reporters looking for information on the party's election strategy, and disseminate press releases and other materials. With experience, communications staffers will be given responsibility for writing and editing press releases and talking points, scheduling media interviews for the committee chairman, and speaking on background with reporters. At the highest level, communications professionals speak on the record with the media and advise candidates and national party leaders on communications strategies.

Finance: Since financial contributions are the lifeblood of politics, the finance departments of the party committees rely on a large staff of fundraisers, and there are many entry-level opportunities available. Inexperienced hires typically work on the administrative aspects of fundraising, such as maintaining databases of donors, tracking mail solicitations, and helping to set up and staff large fundraising events. As fundraisers advance, they receive responsibility for raising money directly from large donors and political action committees, or managing direct mail or phone bank fundraising. At the highest level, fundraisers set financial targets and are responsible for ensuring that fundraising goals are met.

Party committees

Republican National Committee
310 First Street, S.E.
Washington, DC 20003
(202) 863-8500
www.rnc.org

Democratic National Committee
430 S. Capitol Street, S.E.
Washington, DC 20003
(202) 863-8000
www.democrats.org

National Republican Senatorial Committee
425 Second Street, N.E.
Washington, DC 20002
(202) 675-6000
www.nrsc.org

Democratic Senatorial Campaign Committee
120 Maryland Avenue, N.E.
Washington, DC 20002
(202) 224-2447
www.dscc.org

National Republican Congressional Committee
320 First Street, S.E.
Washington, DC 20003
(202) 479-7000
www.nrcc.org

Democrat Congressional Campaign Committee
430 South Capitol Street, S.E.
Washington, DC 20003
(202) 863-1500
www.americashouse.org

Visit Vault at **www.vault.com** for insider company profiles, expert advice,
career message boards, expert resume reviews, the Vault Job Board and more.

VAULT CAREER LIBRARY   83

The Political Track

In addition to the legislative and communications tracks for Hill staffers described in the last chapter, it is worth adding another "track" – that of the political professional. It is a track that Washington's political and policy workers may choose to pursue for a short period of time or for the long term. Those on the political track may start on the Hill, with the party committees and advocacy organization, or may come to Washington from outside the Beltway where they gained experience working on campaigns.

There are two primary sources of employment within Washington for the political track. The party committees (as described above) or with the many consultants that primarily serve political clients. Consultants can be broken roughly into four categories: general consultants, who advise on all matters of campaign strategy, including media, fundraising, research, and organization; advertising consultants, who create television, radio, and direct mail ads; fundraising consultants, who work to raise money for individual candidates by generating donations from Political Action Committees and individuals (for Federal races); and polling consultants, who test the effectiveness of the candidates messages and advise on demographic and other trends. Many of the larger political consultants located in the Washington area hire entry-level positions to assist with administrative tasks and to help coordinate activities on behalf of candidates.

Those starting out on Capitol Hill without much political experience may find a political consultant is worth working for in the short term; however, to move up along the political track, those new to Washington will almost certainly need to get outside the Beltway to work on campaigns. However, it is worth noting that many Capitol Hill staffers have successfully made the transition to the political track after working for Members of Congress, and in particular, by assisting on their election efforts. Additionally, many Hill staffers take a leave of absence during campaign time to work on political campaigns (since Congress is out of session), and thus build their political as well as policy resume.

There are other options for moving up the campaign track, particularly in light of the campaign finance refomr legislation, enatcted into law in 2002, which limits party organizations' abilities to raise funds. This legislation also affects the ability to hire the sane staff levels as in teh past. These options include:

- The AFL-CIO

- U.S. Chamber of Commerce

- National Federation of Independent Businesses

- Sierra Club

- Club for Growth (pro-business)

Lobbying/Government Affairs/Public Affairs

There are a tremendous number of organizations in Washington, DC that seek to influence Congress and the Federal government. Corporations, labor unions, advocacy groups, industry associations and other interests seek to represent their views before Congress and impact the legislative process. Lobbying is carried out in a variety of different ways, but it usually refers to meeting with Members of Congress and their staffs in order to influence legislation or represent a particular point of view. Another way to influence Congress is by using the media, either by placing stories about an issue in a national news outlet or in the hometown media outlets of key Members of Congress.

The influence business in Washington is usually conducted by ex-Members of Congress and Hill staffers, though there are many ways to become involved in the influence business. Large corporations maintain offices in DC employing lobbyists and media relations specialists who work directly for the corporations. There are large law firms and smaller boutique lobbying shops that represent clients on a variety of issues. Advocacy organizations, labor unions, and trade associations also hire lobbyists and public relations professionals.

While popular culture and various good government crusades often find lobbyists an easy target for ridicule, the fact is that lobbying provides an important forum for participation in the democratic process. Influence is big business in Washington, and it provides employment to many people interested and experienced in government and politics.

Visit Vault at **www.vault.com** for insider company profiles, expert advice, career message boards, expert resume reviews, the Vault Job Board and more.

VAULT CAREER LIBRARY   85

Entry-level opportunities

Entry-level opportunities are abundant in the lobbying and public affairs community in Washington, DC. These can be useful for those unable to find a position on the Hill, but who still want to build the necessary experience and contacts to one day work in politics or government. Some people are able to build entire careers in Washington from their start in government relations at one of these organizations without ever working on the Hill in a professional capacity. However, it is widely advised that those ultimately interested in government relations should eventually get Hill experience, even if they don't start there.

In general, the skills and background needed to find a position are very similar: a bachelor's degree, strong writing skills, and organizational ability with a strong preference for some level of experience, either through internships or campaigns.

Law firms and government relations agencies: Law firms and government relations agencies regularly hire college graduates to monitor legislation, attend Congressional hearings, and research public policy issues. These positions are good training grounds for new graduates, and can open many doors. Graduates who begin here can often take on more substantive work than a typical entry-level Capitol Hill staffer would find access to, and can also begin the process of developing a Washington network.

Trade associations: Trade associations represent businesses or organizations with similar interests. Many trade associations are located in Washington, DC since one of the primary responsibilities of these groups is to lobby on behalf of their membership. Examples of large trade associations headquartered in Washington are the National Association of Home Builders and the National Association of Realtors. They hire a variety of government relations professionals, including lobbyists, media relations staff, and Political Action Committee (PAC) directors. Entry-level candidates are hired to assist these functions.

Public relations firms: Public relations agencies serve a variety of clients from their offices in Washington. Of particular interest to readers of this book are the firms that specialize in government affairs work. Many corporations and trade associations hire P.R. agencies to communicate their views on Federal issues to key audiences in the nation's capital utilizing media relations, seminars, speeches, and grassroots communications. Recent college graduates usually enter P.R. firms as junior associates.

Advocacy organizations: There are literally thousands of advocacy organizations in Washington that represent just about every cause imaginable. These are often good starting points for those who are passionate about their own ideologies and agendas. They frequently hire entry-level staffers to assist their government relations and public affairs efforts.

Opportunities for experienced hires

For more experienced hires, the lobbying and government relations world provides an opportunity to use the skills they developed on the Hill but earn more money in the private sector. There is no firm timetable for leaving the Hill or government for the private sector. Some make the leap after a few years of experience; others move over after a full 20-year career on the Hill.

There are several schools of thought on when to make the jump to the private sector. Some advise to stay on the Hill as long as you are moving up and enjoying the work. They recommend that Hill staffers move up as far as they can before taking a private sector position. A long duration on the Hill expands contacts and allows for a greater level of expertise on the workings of Capitol Hill and the machinations of politics – which are well rewarded by those seeking to influence Washington. Others say that it is best to leave before burning out on the Hill. Make the jump before you become too jaded, they argue. You can always go back.

According to several lobbyists, there are a number of factors that employers look for, including:

- **Contacts:** How good are your contacts on the Hill with Members and staff? The higher level your contacts are, the more compensation you will command. Lobbyists especially value staffers with Leadership and Committee experience.

- **Knowledge:** Employers look for people who understand the legislative process, are politically savvy, and who have command of the issues.

- **Relationship building:** Lobbyists must be good at building and growing relationships. Therefore, they should be outgoing, have strong communications skills, and enjoy working with people.

One current lobbyist, who left the Hill after several years as a legislative assistant and legislative director noted that the most successful lobbyists have great sales skills. "In a sense, your are selling your issues to Members of Congress and staff. That means you need to be persuasive and be able to cultivate good relationships. And if you work for a firm, you will be expected

Visit Vault at **www.vault.com** for insider company profiles, expert advice, career message boards, expert resume reviews, the Vault Job Board and more.

VAULT CAREER LIBRARY   87

to go out and try to win business. That can be the hardest aspect of the job for people coming off the Hill, since you have may have to make a lot of unsuccessful pitches for every client you land."

Opportunities for experienced hires are covered in some detail to give those considering either a legislative or communications track an idea of where their experiences can lead in the private sector in Washington, DC (although, as always in the world of Washington, there is substantial cross over and other hidden opportunities).

Lobbying/Government relations

For those coming out of the Legislative track on the Hill or who have significant experience and strong Hill connections, the typical next step is working as a lobbyist, either for a firm, a corporation, a trade association, or an advocacy organization.

For many, the word "lobbyist" conjures images of men in thousand-dollar suits wooing politicians with wads of campaign cash. Despite the stereotypes, lobbying plays an important role in the legislative process.

What most people don't realize is that they are most likely represented by several lobbyists. If they work for a corporation, their employer almost certainly has a team of lobbyists in Washington to help the company grow and provide employment. If they are members of a union, their dues finance a large lobbying and political advocacy operation. If they are a member of an interest group or membership organization, such as the Sierra Club, the U.S. Chamber of Commerce, or the National Rifle Association, they have lobbyists looking after issues that affect their memberships. Virtually every conceivable group or interest is represented in some way before Congress.

Lobbyists are either employees of these organizations or they work as consultants. They develop expertise in the issues on which they lobby and help inform Members and their staffs on the positions of their clients or employers. They attempt to influence Members to pass legislation favorable to their employer or client. In general, lobbyists work in one of four environments: as consultants at a firm or as employees of a trade association, corporation, or advocacy organization. While much of their responsibility will be similar regardless of who they work for, there are several key differences, as highlighted below.

Law firms: Large law firms, small government relations firms, and even some public relations firms hire ex-Capitol Hill staffers to lobby on behalf of a set of clients. Firms typically provide the highest monetary compensation, but hours can be long and there is often a strong pressure to develop new business. Those who enjoy working on a variety of different issues and enjoy the opportunity to interact with a broad group of clients will do best at firms. Additionally, lobbyists at firms must be entrepreneurial, since they will be expected to help bring in business to the firm. This is especially true at smaller firms, which provide the opportunity for those who successfully bring in new business to increase their compensation quickly. Some of the larger firms with a strong Washington presence include Akin Gump, Arent Fox, and Wiley Rein and Fielding, but there are many, many firms that do significant government and lobbying work.

Trade associations: Trade associations represent companies in a specific business or industry, and provide a variety of services to their members, including lobbying. Lobbyists at trade associations will receive good pay (but less than at a firm) and generally have reasonable hours, except when a particularly hot issue in their industry is percolating in Congress. These lobbyists will have a narrower range of issues that they work on, since the greatest lobbying efforts will be placed on those issues most pertinent to the industry.

Corporations: Individual corporations hire lobbyists as employees. These lobbyists specifically represent their employer on Capitol Hill and work on those issues most important to the corporation. As with trade associations, the hours are generally better than working for a firm, although the monetary compensation is usually lower. Lobbyists for corporations often receive stock options and other employee benefits. Corporate lobbyists also spend a great deal of time working with individuals inside corporations, including senior management, and less time on Capitol Hill as compared with many of their colleagues.

Advocacy organizations: Advocacy organizations hire lobbyists to represent their causes before Congress. Advocacy organizations pay less than other employers, but they do provide the opportunity to work on specific issues that their lobbyists are passionate about. Advocacy organizations exist on the right and left of American politics, so regardless of which party a lobbyist comes from, there are certain to be opportunities.

Visit Vault at www.vault.com for insider company profiles, expert advice, career message boards, expert resume reviews, the Vault Job Board and more

VAULT CAREER LIBRARY   89

A Day in the Life of a Lobbyist

8:30 a.m.: Arrive early to read the papers and look over the schedule for today.

9:00 a.m.: Meet with colleagues to run through the lobbying schedule for the week. This is a good time to leverage their contacts on the Hill on behalf of your clients.

10:00 a.m.: Take a cab up to Capitol Hill to meet with staff members on behalf of several clients. A good portion of the day is typically spent outside the office, especially for lobbyists with a firm.

10:30 a.m.: Meet with a several legislative assistants to Members serving on the House Transportation and Infrastructure Committee on behalf of a client looking to encourage Members of Congress to support a particular piece of legislation.

12:00 p.m.: Take a senior Senate staff member to lunch. Meals are a huge part of the job since they are a great opportunity to build and maintain relationships with key Hill contacts.

1:00 p.m.: Back to the Hill to meet with more staff members.

3:00 p.m.: Return to the office. Must spend some time scheduling appointments for the rest of the week on behalf of clients.

4:00 p.m.: Participate in a conference call with a client that wants to ensure its project is funded in the upcoming appropriations process.

5:00 p.m.: Start putting together a pitch for a new business presentation at the end of the week.

6:30 p.m.: Meet a former Hill colleague for dinner – yet another night at one of DC's swank downtown steak houses to talk a little business and stay in touch.

Opportunities for Law Students/JDs

CHAPTER 9

For law students, the nation's capital offers an astounding array of options that can provide access to some truly unique opportunities. Like most large cities, Washington, DC is home to many law firms, from small boutiques to large international firms. Law students will also find opportunities unavailable elsewhere, including the chance to work on public policy as a staff member on Capitol Hill, as an attorney for the Federal government, or as an in-house counsel for an interest group or trade association. These experiences can lead to one of the ultimate power positions in DC, the lawyer-lobbyist.

For graduating law students, there are several paths into the political realm of Washington. The most common entry points are:

- Joining a law firm

- Finding a position with the executive branch of the Federal government

- Going to work on the Hill

Each option has its own unique advantages and disadvantages, depending on what the individual student hopes to accomplish. However, the same factors that are true for undergrads apply to law students. Building contacts and experience is the key to opening many future career doors.

Joining a Law Firm

While some argue that the best way to begin a career in Washington in government and politics is to go directly to work in the executive branch or on Capitol Hill, others stress that joining a firm can be a very effective way to build a Washington career.

Joining a firm out of school has some clear advantages over going directly to the Hill or accepting a position with the Federal government. For one, it provides graduates with a higher salary than they would receive in a government positions. This is important, since most law school graduates accumulate a significant amount of debt pursuing their education. Another is the opportunity to work alongside partners and senior attorneys with significant Washington experience. Since Washington's revolving career door usually opens to lucrative private sector experience after a successful

Visit Vault at **www.vault.com** for insider company profiles, expert advice, career message boards, expert resume reviews, the Vault Job Board and more.

V∧ULT CAREER LIBRARY   91

career in government, many of the highest-level attorneys in Washington law firms have held senior positions on the Hill or with the executive branch, including chief counsel positions with Congressional committees or assistant secretary positions for an administration. At firms, new lawyers will have the opportunity to work directly with these senior attorneys and benefit from their experience, and possibly their rolodexes.

However, joining a firm does have some downsides that the politically ambitious need to consider. Building a strong network will be more challenging than it would in a position on the Hill or with the Federal government. The hours will be longer and the downtown locations of most law firms will be a barrier to many of the social activities Hill staffers use to build their networks. Additionally, there is no guarantee that initial assignments will necessarily provide access to top senior partners or to assignments of specific interest. Therefore, those pursuing the firm route will need to take extra steps to building their networks by socializing with Hill and government staffers, joining appropriate professional organizations, and making efforts to become involved in the political process by attending fundraisers or volunteering for campaigns and other political activities.

With the right set of contacts and some solid experience, attorneys at firms can choose to then pursue positions with Congress or with the Executive branch. However, they must be prepared to take a pay cut, but with the knowledge that their experience will one day pay off when they leave government and return to the private sector.

Says one attorney who began with a firm, moved to the Hill, and now is a political appointee for the Bush administration: "I tell all lawyers I talk with not to discount going to a firm, even if your real passion is for Capitol Hill. The contacts you make can be extraordinary. In my firm alone, we have a former FEC [Federal Election Commission] commissioner and several assistant secretaries." However, he cautions that lawyers at firms will need to pull double duty to move in politics: "The challenge for any lawyer at a firm is to build their network even as they work downtown. Live on Capitol Hill and hang out with Hill staffers after work and on weekends. If you have a friend from college working on Capitol Hill, make sure to stay in touch and get to know all his friends. With the right networking, when the right opportunity comes along, you will be ready to take it."

Federal Government – Executive Branch

The Federal government employs more than 25,000 attorneys, many of them in Washington, DC. These lawyers work on an assortment of issues and for employers as diverse as the Department of Defense and the Equal Employment Opportunity Commission. Starting positions can be stepping-stones to a career with the Federal government, government relations, or someday to partnership in a law firm.

The Department of Justice is seen as one of the premier agencies for attorneys to work for. Other popular agencies include those that issue regulations, such as the Securities and Exchange Commission, the Environmental Protection Agency, and the Department of Energy, to name just a few. For those with interest in a specific area of the law, the Federal government provides an appropriate venue to build their skills, make contacts, and contribute to the political and policy-making process.

These positions are popular because of the tremendous experience they provide, not because they pay well. Those admitted to the program typically start at the GS-11 level (in Federal government bureaucrat-speak, GS-11 translates into a range of roughly $42,900 to $55,873 for 2003). Specifics tend to vary by program and department, so please use the contacts provided for current salary levels, application procedures, and employment details.

The Department of Justice

The United States Department of Justice bills itself as the nation's largest law firm, employing approximately 9,200 attorneys nationwide. The Department of Justice serves as counsel for the citizens of the United States. It prosecutes criminals, ensures the integrity of the nation's free market economic system, protects consumers from fraud and other forms of abuse, and enforces drug, immigration and naturalization laws. It also represents the government of the United States before the Supreme Court. The head of the Department, the Attorney General, advises the President and other key executive branch personnel on legal matters.

Employment with the Department of Justice is highly competitive; in 2002 nearly 5,000 law students applied for approximately 150 slots in the Department's honors program. Those wishing to begin their careers with the Department can enter through only a few select channels: by gaining

Visit Vault at **www.vault.com** for insider company profiles, expert advice, career message boards, expert resume reviews, the Vault Job Board and more.

VAULT CAREER LIBRARY   93

experience through an internship or applying through the Department's honors program.

The honors program is the Department's recruitment program for entry-level attorneys (most departments have honors programs to recruit attorneys from law school; please see below for additional details). It is the only vehicle by which the Department hires graduating law students. It is highly competitive and has a detailed application process. Eligibility is determined by three criteria, which generally are (contact the Department or look at the web site for specifics at www.usdoj.gov):

- Third-year law students; or

- Full-time graduate law students in their final year of study; or

- Judicial law clerks serving prior to the application deadline (and generally no more than nine months post graduation).

Additionally, the Department offers a competitive summer internship program for second year law students (please check eligibility requirements with the DOJ for exceptions). Eight organizations within the Department formally participate in the Summer Law Intern Program: Antitrust Division; Civil Division; Civil Rights Division; Environment and Natural Resources Division; Tax Division; Federal Bureau of Prisons; the Executive Office for Immigration Review; Immigration and Naturalization Service. Interning for the Department can lead to an offer of full-time employment upon graduation.

Honors programs

In addition to the Department of Justice, many other departments offer similar opportunities through honors programs for graduating law students and internship opportunities for those still in school.

Law school career offices should have extensive information on the internship and full-time career opportunities available to law students. Application procedures and requirements vary by department. Below is a selection of some of the specific recruitment programs available and links to get additional information:

Central Intelligence Agency
- The CIA's Legal Honors Program provides a three year introduction to the practice of national security law. The Office of the General Counsel handles legal issues relating to foreign intelligence and counterintelligence activities, international terrorism, and other international security issues.

Information on the program, including application information, is available at www.cia.gov/ogc/honors/htm.

- The CIA runs a small and select Summer Legal Clerk Program for law students to obtain broad exposure to the practice of intelligence law. Information on the program, including application materials and deadlines, is available at: www.cia.gov/ogc/summer/htm.

Commerce Department (Office of the General Counsel)

- Summer internships and full-time positions can be found at the Office of General Counsel's web site, www.ogc.doc.gov under vacancies. Internships are offered throughout the Department's eight bureaus and are open to first and second year law students.

Education Department

- Summer internships: www.ed.gov/offices/oiia/internships/index.html.

Environmental Protection Agency

- For internship or entry-level legal positions, attorneys apply directly to the office at which they are interested in working (including the Washington, DC headquarters). Information on applying can be found at: www.epa.gov/epahome/jobs.htm.

Equal Employment Opportunity Commission

- Full-time hires from law school are made through the honors program. Information on the honors program can be found on the commission's web site at www.eeoc.gov.

- Summer internships are available at the Washington, DC headquarters and in the commission's many field offices, which can also be found at the commission's web site.

Federal Bureau of Investigations

- Summer internships are available by applying through the FBI's honors program, which hires both undergraduate and graduate students. Information is available at www.fbi.gov./employment/honors/htm.

- Full-time opportunities are can be explored at the FBI's web site, though attorney positions are not specifically broken out from others.

Federal Election Commission

- Those interested in summer clerkships or full-time entry-level positions can find a downloadable brochure at www.fec.gov/jobs.htm.

Visit Vault at **www.vault.com** for insider company profiles, expert advice, career message boards, expert resume reviews, the Vault Job Board and more.

VAULT CAREER LIBRARY   **95**

Federal Trade Commission

- Information on both full-time opportunities through the honors program and the commission's internship program for second-year law students can be found on the commission's web site, www.ftc.gov.

Housing and Urban Development Department

- The Legal Honors Intern program is the only recruitment vehicle for hiring graduating law students into HUD. Interns are assigned to a one-year legal internship; following the completion of their internships they may be granted offers of permanent employment. Additional information on the program can be found at www.hud.gov/jobs/index.cfm.

Interior Department

- The Solicitor's Honors Program is the principal means of entry-level hiring for Interior lawyers. New attorneys are hired for a one year internship program, after which they may be offered permanent employment based on their performance. Information on the program is available at www.doi.gov/sol/sohonpgm.html.

Internal Revenue Service

- The IRS runs a Summer Law Intern Program for law students interested in tax law. Offers of permanent employment may be made to some second-year students. Information on the program can be found at www.jobs.irs.gov.

- The Chief Counsel's Honors Program is designed to recruit graduating law students. Lawyers begin their careers at the IRS as law clerks before becoming members of the bar and assuming permanent positions. Information on the program is available at www.jobs.irs.gov.

Labor Department

- The Office of the Solicitor, which employs 500 attorneys, is responsible for enforcing occupational safety and health laws, certain civil rights laws, minimum wage and overtime laws, and many other labor laws. Attorneys hired into the honors program spend two years in the Special Appellate and Supreme Court Litigation Division before being assigned to another division in Washington. Information on the program is available at www.gov/sol/honorsprogram.htm.

Securities and Exchange Commission

- The Securities and Exchange Commission bills itself as "the investor's advocate" and describes its primary mission as protecting investors and maintaining the integrity of the securities markets. The SEC hires graduating law students, LLMs, and judicial law clerks as entry-level attorneys under the "Advanced Commitment Program," primarily to its Washington, DC headquarters. Information on the program is available at www.sec.gov/jobs.

- The Summer Honors program gives first- and second-year law students the opportunity to work side by side with Commission lawyers. The program allows for assignments in Washington, DC and the Commission's 11 regional and district offices. Information on the program is available at www.sec.gov/jobs.

Transportation Department

- The Department of Transportation develops national transportation goals and policies and coordinates the Federal transportation program. The Department's Honors Attorneys programs recruits 10 graduating law students to a two-year rotational program. These candidates are given top priority in filling vacant legal positions within the department. Application information can be found at www.dot.gov/ost/ogc.

- Several departments within the Office of General Council offer unpaid legal internship during the summer and throughout the year. Application information is available at the web site.

Treasury Department

- The U.S. Department of Treasury hires graduating law students, LLMs, and judicial clerks through its two-year honors program. The Department offers honors program participants the opportunity to rotate throughout the Department or focus in one of three areas: banking and finance, international affairs, or legislation and litigation oversight. Information on the program is available at www.ustreas.gov/offices/general-counsel.

- The Department also offers an Honors Program Summer Clerkship for law students. Honors clerks are generally not compensated. Application information can be found at the web site.

Federal Government – Capitol Hill

Law students interested in working for the legislative branch will want to consider positions with Members of Congress and Committees. These positions, such as a professional legislative staff member to a Committee or as a legislative aide to a Member of Congress, provide solid experience and can be stepping-stones to higher-level political positions or to careers with lobbying firms or government relations offices of major corporations.

Visit Vault at **www.vault.com** for insider company profiles, expert advice, career message boards, expert resume reviews, the Vault Job Board and more.

VAULT CAREER LIBRARY 97

Like undergrads, law students will need to build experience prior to graduation to have the best chance at competitive Hill positions. One way to build experience is to work for a few years on Capitol Hill before returning to law school. Many people interested in both politics and the law find that working for some time on Capitol Hill helps sharpen their interest in the law, and more specifically, on the area of law that they would like to concentrate on. Those law students who have not had the opportunity to serve on Capitol Hill prior to attending law school will most likely need to build experience through internships prior to graduation if they wish to pursue a position there upon graduation. Please note that even for law students, many Hill internships are unpaid or offer only a small stipend.

One popular option for those interested in a Washington career in government and law is to attend one of the local evening law programs while working full time on the Hill. There are five major law schools within the Washington, DC region offering night programs: Georgetown University; George Washington University; Catholic University, American University, and George Mason University.

Depending on the extent of their Hill experience, law school graduates can start on the Hill as a professional staff member for a Committee or as a legislative aide with a member of the House of Representatives or a Senator. As with the positions in the Federal government, starting salaries will be much less than law school graduates would earn with a firm, so they will need to consider their debt load in deciding to pursue opportunities on the Hill.

With significant Hill experience, however, lawyers will find themselves much in demand in private sector government affairs positions, usually with a lobbying firm or a government relations office of a corporation.

Government Affairs/Lobbying

While many law students are interested in moving directly into lobbying, gaining experience on Capitol Hill, either with a Committee or a Member's office, is crucial to finding such a position. However, attorneys who gain Hill experience usually find their skills and experience to be very highly valued in the private sector.

Private firms also hire lawyers with Hill experience, particularly those with experience in a specific issue area, such as labor law or federal communications policies. For more information, see the prior discussion of public affairs and lobbying.

It is worth noting again that a law degree is not a prerequisite for a career in government affairs or lobbying. Many lobbyists do not have a law degree. However, it can be helpful in terms of drafting specific language and providing attorney client privilege during strategy discussions.

Interest Groups and Trade Associations

Many Washington, DC interest groups and trade associations maintain in-house counsel. These positions offer law students the best of both worlds: the chance to work on a specific issue or policy area with the benefits of an in-house lifestyle. For many of these positions, lawyers will need some level of Capitol Hill, government, or regulatory experience.

Interest groups and trade association counsels work on a variety of issues not related to lobbying. The best way to identify general counsel positions is to examine trade associations related to a particular industry or to look for positions with advocacy organizations that deal with a specific issue of interest.

According to one counsel with a Virginia-based trade association: "While the pay is less than most first-year associates make at a large law firm, I have an interesting set of issues that cover policy and business considerations. I have the opportunity to work with senior executives from our member companies and the Federal government. It's intellectually stimulating work, and I still get home before 6 p.m. on most nights."

Visit Vault at **www.vault.com** for insider company profiles, expert advice, career message boards, expert resume reviews, the Vault Job Board and more.

VAULT CAREER LIBRARY   99

Opportunities for MBAs

Washington, DC has largely been an untapped source of career opportunities for business school students and MBAs. However, several recent trends indicate that MBAs may start looking to Washington for positions not available elsewhere. These trends include a heightened interest in employment with nonprofits and a burgeoning effort by some Federal agencies to recruit MBAs. Additionally, there are MBA employers that exist only in Washington, such as the World Bank.

Despite increased interest in hiring MBAs by many of these employers, in general, these organizations have limited and spotty recruiting efforts on business school campuses. The onus remains on interested students to research appropriate opportunities and network with individuals with similar interests. The section below contains a guide to several of the employment options for MBAs in Washington along with advice on how to identify opportunities and successfully apply for positions.

Federal Government

Washington, DC is slowly, but increasingly, becoming more aware of the benefits of the MBA as well as the need to bring in qualified managers with more than just government experience. When George W. Bush was sworn in as the 43rd President of the United States, he was commonly referred to as the "MBA President," since, as a graduate of the Harvard Business School he is the first chief executive of the United States to hold the degree. Several of his appointments to fill key administration posts were also MBAs, including Elaine Chao, the Secretary of Labor, who received her MBA from the Harvard Business School and Don Evans, the Secretary of Commerce, who received an MBA from the University of Texas. Many other of his top appointments were culled from the world of business, including Paul O'Neil, his first Secretary of the Treasury and former CEO of Alcoa, as well as his replacement, John Snow, who was the head of CSX Corp.

The change at the top has not translated yet into widespread opportunities for MBAs, but the government has grown more receptive to MBAs as it begins to appreciate the skills and capabilities they bring to bear. For example, there have been recent efforts to recruit on MBA campuses. In the 2003 recruiting season, the U.S. Department of the Treasury has visited select campuses seeking to fill internships and full-time positions. At times, the CIA has promoted opportunities with MBA programs and advertised for MBAs as part

Visit Vault at **www.vault.com** for insider company profiles, expert advice, career message boards, expert resume reviews, the Vault Job Board and more.

VAULT CAREER LIBRARY   101

of its financial analysis teams on popular job posting sites, such as HotJobs.com and *The Washington Post*.

In 2002, Secretary Chao of the U.S. Department of Labor launched an initiative specifically to recruit MBAs to the Department. With a large proportion of senior Department personnel scheduled to retire in the coming years, Secretary Chao moved aggressively to create a new pipeline of talent and specifically identified hiring MBAs as the future of the Department.

Finding a position with the Federal government

As would be expected with the Federal government, bureaucracy rules the hiring process. However, as with any organization, there are paths around the human resources quagmire. MBAs interested in finding an appropriate position with the Federal government should apply the tools emphasized by any career counseling office: Identify your interests, find out the general requirements for position, network, and utilize internships.

Since the Federal government is required to post nearly all vacancies, one potential resource to use in identifying appropriate opportunities is its career listing web site, www.usacareers.com. However, a word of warning: while the site provides a useful starting point and a valuable research tool, using it exclusively for a job search with the Federal government would sell your efforts short. Instead, for MBAs it can be best used as means to examine the types of positions available and the general salary ranges. Still, even the position descriptions can be overly bureaucratic, and therefore the site should only be considered a starting point in the research process.

According to several MBAs employed by the Federal government in Washington, the best way to identify opportunities is by networking with those already working there and with those in the nonprofits and other entities that regularly partner or interact with the Federal agencies. Two good ways to make such contacts are through MBA alumni networks and student or school sponsored conferences focusing on the public sector and non-profit management.

Applying for positions can also be highly bureaucratic, and again, interested applicants are well advised to use their networks to begin the application process. While all applicants must eventually go through the human resources department to determine whether they are qualified and if so, their pay level, it is far more fruitful to begin the application process with the office one wishes to join than with the human resources department. This is where networking can pay off, since ultimately hiring decisions are made within a specific office for high-level candidates. In fact, many government managers already have an applicant in mind before a position is posted.

One MBA graduate who turned to the Federal government after graduation says that while finding a government position can take effort, the MBA is definitely seen as a benefit. "There are a lot of hiring managers who will be receptive to talking with MBAs simply because they hold the credential," he says. "MBAs with a specific interest should seek out managers in the Federal government, send them their resumes, and then try to follow up."

The insider also confirmed that there is a growing awareness of the value of an MBA, but that the government hasn't been fast enough to quickly establish the right recruiting policies to bring more business students into the Federal workforce. "The fact of the matter is that the government just doesn't pay what the private sector does," he says. "But, for those with a strong interest in government work, there are many ways in and many rewarding career paths."

Areas of interest to MBAs

Since most MBAs aren't interested in becoming lifetime bureaucrats, they usually consider specific opportunities in order to gain the experience they need to advance in their chosen professions. The following are areas of the Federal government that provide career enhancing opportunities:

Community and economic development

Community and economic development is an area that has captured the interest of MBAs. Since community and economic development is often the result of cooperation among public sector, private sector, and non-profit entities, a position with the Federal government can be an effective way to build experience, gain contacts within the development community, and gain an understanding of the government's role in community and economic development and the resources it makes available.

There are several agencies within the Federal government that have community and economic development functions. These include the U.S. Department of Treasury, the U.S. Department of Commerce, and the Small Business Administration. Since roles within each agency will vary with the specific mission of the department, interested candidates should try to learn about each department's operations and opportunities through networking with organizations such as Net Impact, alumni, and by contacting hiring managers directly to discuss opportunities.

Visit Vault at **www.vault.com** for insider company profiles, expert advice, career message boards, expert resume reviews, the Vault Job Board and more

VAULT CAREER LIBRARY   103

Management

There are many opportunities within the Federal government for MBAs to gain management experience. However, these opportunities must be ferreted out, and will depend on what the MBA hopes to gain by joining the Federal government. For example, an MBA with an interest in the Federal budget process could attempt to locate an analyst position with the Office of Management and Budget. Another potential source of management positions will be the newly created Department of Homeland Security. Since the Homeland Security Department will be free of some of the Federal employment regulations imposed on virtually every other Federal entity, there may be more opportunities for MBAs to utilize their management abilities to a greater degree than elsewhere in the Federal bureaucracy. MBAs need to think creatively about how their skills relate to government management. Since the Department of Homeland Security is being created from programs and agencies run by a variety of Federal entities, it could be thought of in business terms as a "post-merger integration project." (As of this writing, the Department of Homeland is still being formed. Openings, as they are identified, are posted at the Federal government's employment site, www.usajobs.opm.gov.)

One avenue for MBAs into the Federal government is through the Presidential Management Internship (PMI) program, which is open to all students pursuing master's or doctoral degrees. To be considered for the program, students must submit an application and be nominated by the dean, chairperson, or program director of their academic program. Once accepted, PMIs must find an appropriate position within the Federal government. The program lasts two years, with PMIs beginning at the GS-9 level (approximately $35,500 to $46,100. After one year, they are eligible for promotion to the GS-11 level ($42,900 to $55,800). At the end of the program, PMI program participants may be converted to a permanent position with the Federal government and are eligible for the GS-12 grade level ($51,500 to $66,900). For detailed information on the program, see its web site at www.pmi.opm.gov.

Additionally, the Department of Labor has begun to actively recruit MBAs for general management positions with strong results. For 2002, its first year in operation, the Department's MBA recruitment program reported receiving more than 250 applications for thirty openings. While MBAs start at the GS-9 level, the Department is offering other incentives, including recruitment bonuses and loan forgiveness programs.

Upon acceptance into the program, MBAs will be allowed to rotate through several different assignments before being placed in a permanent position.

The permanent assignments are based on the needs of the Department and the long-term interests of each participant.

A senior official working on the program glows about its initial results: "We didn't know what to expect when we fist put the program into place, but we have been very pleased with the results. In fact, several other offices within the Federal government have approached us about putting up similar recruitment programs for themselves."

Application information is available on the Department's web site at www.dol.gov.

International development

The Federal government also provides options for MBA students interested in international development, a field that has traditionally and still remains dominated by economists.

Since there are no formal recruitment programs in place for MBAs for international development positions with the Federal government. Interested students will have to network with both on-campus and outside organizations to uncover opportunities.

The U.S. Department of Treasury's Office of International Affairs often recruits MBAs for financial analysis positions covering such issues as debt policy or international trade. It particularly is interested in MBAs with strong experience in the banking and financial service sector as well as international experience. The office's recruitment efforts include posting position openings with MBA career offices and general advertising.

Nonprofits

As more and more MBA students continue to turn to the non-profit world, Washington will become an increasingly popular destination. Many of the largest nonprofits, including the United Way, the American Red Cross, and the AARP are located in the Washington region.

As with other opportunities in Washington, networking is the best way to identify appropriate positions since many positions are not advertised and most nonprofits don't have the resources to recruit on campuses. MBA clubs focused on the non-profit world, such as Net Impact, provide outstanding networking opportunities through volunteer activities. (While not specifically Washington focused, the Net Impact job board does often have opportunities in the Washington metro area.) Good sources for identifying opportunities with Washington, DC nonprofits include:

Visit Vault at **www.vault.com** for insider company profiles, expert advice, career message boards, expert resume reviews, the Vault Job Board and more.

VAULT CAREER LIBRARY   **105**

- *The Washington Post* job listings at www.washingtonpost.com.

- The MBA-Nonprofit Connection: mnc.nonprofitoffice.com

- www.net-impact.org

International Finance Organizations

Washington, DC plays host to many organizations established specifically to assist in international finance and development. With international development an area of intense interest for MBAs who wish to apply their business expertise to improve conditions around the globe, Washington is a natural destination to search for opportunities. Increasingly, positions with these international finance organizations are becoming good opportunities for MBAs.

World Bank

The World Bank Group is a major source of assistance to developing nations around the world. In 2002, it provided more than $19.5 billion in loans to client countries and works in more than 100 developing economies. It is funded by 184 member countries, which act as the shareholders of the bank and direct its activities.

There are five closely associated institutions comprising the World Bank Group: the International Bank for Reconstruction and Development (IBRD), the International Development Association (IDA), the International Finance Corporation, the Multilateral Investment Guarantee Agency, and the International Centre for Settlement of Investment Disputes. The "World Bank" specifically includes two of those groups, the IDA and the IBRD.

The World Bank helps fight poverty around the world by applying both financial resources and expertise to help developing countries become more financially stable and self-sufficient. The bank assists poor countries by investing in people through health care and educational initiatives, and notes that it is the largest external funder for both education programs and AIDS/HIV prevention globally. In 2002, it provided more than $19.5 billion in loans to client countries and works in more than 100 developing economies. Additionally, the World Bank focuses on building strong institutions and government as a means of addressing poverty. It supports private business development as well as governmental reforms to create a stable economic development that encourages investment and long-term planning.

The World Bank is a prestigious employer. Its Young Professionals program provides a starting point for employment, including MBAs. It includes two rotational assignments in different departments. The purpose of the program is to prepare a select group of individuals for permanent positions within the World Bank. It is an extremely competitive program. Those MBAs interested in joining the program must stand out among thousands of applicants for about 40 openings.

The Young Professionals program is open to master's degree holders in a variety of areas, including business, but also economics, education, social sciences, engineering, education, and other areas. Candidates must be under 32 years old and should have foreign work and language experience.

Information on the program is available at the World Bank web site, www.worldbank.org.

International Finance Corporation (IFC)

The International Finance Corporation (IFC), which is part of the World Bank Group, offers career opportunities to MBAs interested in pursuing positions in international finance. If you believe that private sector investment is a major tool in the global fight against poverty, then the IFC deserves a serious look.

The IFC promotes private sector investment as a way to reduce poverty in developing nations and improve the lives of their citizens. In fact it is the largest multilateral source of loan and equity financing for private sector projects in developing countries. The IFC provides three primary services:

• Financing private sector projects in the developing world.

• Helping private companies in the developing world access financing in the international financial markets.

• Providing advice and technical assistance to businesses and governments.

The IFC recruits at select MBA programs across the country to fill positions for its Global Transaction Team, a rotational program for freshly minted MBAs. In 2002, 12 MBAs joined the Global Transaction Team from several of the world's top business schools. Participants typically rotate throughout the IFC's matrix system, gaining experience in functional areas such as Oil, Gas and Mining; Agri-business; or Manufacturing, or in geographic regions

Visit Vault at **www.vault.com** for insider company profiles, expert advice, career message boards, expert resume reviews, the Vault Job Board and more.

VAULT CAREER LIBRARY   107

like Asia or Latin America. After a few rotations, members of the program typically are brought into one particular area to continue their careers at the IFC.

MBAs joining the IFC will find the work to be similar to an associate level investment banker or an associate at a private equity firm. Often, they will work with investment banks in arranging financing packages, which vary in size but utilize primarily debt instruments. There are, however, several key differences. According to one participant, the IFC offers associate level employees the opportunity to be more involved in the deal flow than would be possible at a large investment bank. And while there will be less hours than at an investment bank, the compensation is also lower.

MBAs interested in applying for the Global Transaction Team should be prepared to emphasize the following in their application materials and interviews:

- **Transactional finance experience:** Positions on the Global Transaction team are very transactional, and generally require prior experience in finance;

- **International development interest:** Candidates must exhibit a strong interest in international development and should have relevant international experience; and

- **International experience and language skills:** Strong knowledge of developing regions and fluency in more than one language are seen as beneficial in the hiring process.

The IFC also takes experienced hires. However, there is no formal recruitment mechanism for those interested in joining the IFC mid career. Opportunities are posted to the web site at www.ifc.org/careers.

The International Monetary Fund (IMF)

The International Monetary Fund was established by its member nations to promote international monetary cooperation, exchange stability and to foster economic growth and strong economies. The IMF has been likened to a doctor for the world's economies. It monitors its members' economic health, and where appropriate, can take steps to nurse ailing countries back to their feet. The IMF carries out its mission by monitoring economic and financial developments around the globe, providing loans to countries, and assisting in policy development.

While the IMF typically hires economists, insiders suggest that it has stepped up its recruitment of MBAs for its analyst program. While the analyst program requires candidates with at least a BA, most candidates possess master's degrees. MBAs, particularly those with a background in economics and significant coursework in finance, have been recruited to fill specific needs at the IMF, such as monitoring and analyzing world financial markets. Since senior members of the IMF are almost exclusively PhD economists, those at the analyst level tend to work at the IMF for a few years before moving on to other positions or returning to academia.

For those interested in positions at the IMF, the best route is of course networking. Options for networking include alumni (both business school and undergraduate) and by making contact with current IMF personnel (including informational interviews). Positions are also posted on its web site, www.imf.org.

Inter-American Development Bank (IDB)

The Inter-American Development Bank was established to help accelerate economic development in Latin America and the Caribbean. In addition to the bank, the Inter-American Development Bank Group includes the Inter-American Investment Corporation (IIC) and the Multilateral Investment Fund (MIF). The IIC is an autonomous affiliate of the bank that promotes economic development by financing small- and medium-sized private enterprises. The MIF promotes private sector development.

The bank has two principal objectives: reducing poverty and promoting environmentally sustainable growth. To attain these objectives, the bank works in four priority areas:

- Supporting policies and programs that foster development within the Latin American and Caribbean region.

- Strengthening the efficiency and transparency of public institutions.

- Investing in social programs that expand opportunities for the poor.

- Forging links among countries in the region.

The IDB recruits master's candidates through its Young Professionals program. Information on the program is available at www.iadb.org. The IIC and MIF also have employment information on their sites, which can be accessed through the IADB site.

Visit Vault at **www.vault.com** for insider company profiles, expert advice, career message boards, expert resume reviews, the Vault Job Board and more.

VAULT CAREER LIBRARY   **109**

About the Author

William McCarthy

William McCarthy, MBA (Wharton), has worked for approximately 10 years in Washington with national political party organizations, as well as a large public affairs/government relations agency.

Visit Vault at **www.vault.com** for insider company profiles, expert advice, career message boards, expert resume reviews, the Vault Job Board and more.

VAULT CAREER LIBRARY   111

Use the Internet's
MOST TARGETED
job search tools.

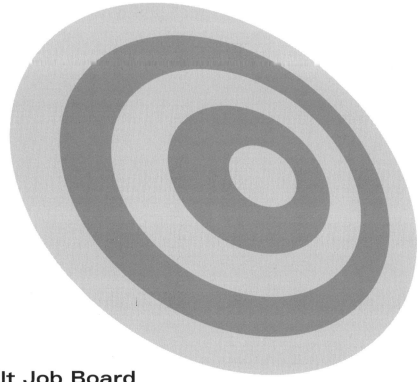

Vault Job Board

Target your search by industry, function, and experience level, and find the job openings that you want.

VaultMatch Resume Database

Vault takes match-making to the next level: post your resume and customize your search by industry, function, experience and more. We'll match job listings with your interests and criteria and e-mail them directly to your inbox.